$11 85

INTERACTIONS I
A Writing Process Book

INTERACTIONS I
A Writing Process Book

Margaret Keenan Segal
Stevens Institute of Technology

Cheryl Pavlik
Columbia University

RANDOM HOUSE New York

This book was developed for Random House by Eirik Børve, Inc.

Library of Congress Cataloging in Publication Data

Pavlik, Cheryl, 1949–
    Interactions 1.   A writing process book.

    1. English language—Text-books for foreign speakers.
2. English language—Composition and exercises.
I. Segal, Margaret, 1950–   . II. Title.
PE1128.P368   1985   808'.042   85–1841
ISBN 0-394-33697-6
Manufactured in the United States of America

Text design and production: Donna Davis
Cover design: Cheryl Carrington
Cover photo: Peter Menzel
Drawings: Axelle Fortier
Photo research: Lindsay Kefauver

Photo Credits

p. 12, Saxon Donnelly/Courtesy University of California, Berkeley; p. 17,
Courtesy, Museum of Fine Arts, Boston, Gift of Mrs. George van Lengerke
Meyer; p. 19, Courtesy of The Art Institute of Chicago; p. 20, The Prado
Museum, Madrid. Photo: Alinari/Art Resource; p. 22, Kunsthistorisches
Museum, Vienna. Photo: Saskia/Art Resource; p. 25, Rijksmuseum-
Stichting, Amsterdam; p. 27, Ed Buryn/Jeroboam, Inc.; p. 33, Jerry
Howard/Stock, Boston; p. 46, Ellis Herwig/Stock, Boston; p. 49, Fritz
Photography/FPG; p. 75 and 82, Charles Kennard/Stock, Boston; p. 75 and
87, Gregg Mancuso/Stock, Boston; p. 75, Peter Simon/Stock, Boston; p. 75,
Courtesy, Mount Zion Hospital and Medical Center, San Francisco; p. 80,
Suzanne Arms/Jeroboam, Inc.; p. 83, Kay Lawson/Jeroboam, Inc.; p. 90 and
91, Culver Pictures, Inc.; p. 93, © 1982 Universal City Studios, Inc.; p. 96,
Copyright © Lucasfilm Ltd. 1982. All rights reserved; p. 117, Dan Budnik/
Woodfin Camp & Associates; Arthur Tress/Magnum Photos, Inc.; Elliott
Erwitt/Magnum Photos, Inc.; Robert Azzi/Woodfin Camp & Associates; p.
121, Hank Lebo/Jeroboam, Inc.; p. 125, Bob Clay/Jeroboam, Inc.; p. 126,
Jane Scherr/Jeroboam, Inc.; pg. 129, Erich Hartmann/Magnum Photos,
Inc.; p. 130, Jean-Claude Lejeune/Stock, Boston; p. 135, Cary Wolinsky/
Stock, Boston; Tom Cheek/Stock, Boston; p. 137, Peter Menzel/Stock,
Boston; p. 141, Don Ivers/Jeroboam, Inc.

CONTENTS

Chapter 5   HOUSING AND THE FAMILY   52

Rhetorical focus: autobiographical narration
Grammatical and stylistic focus: past tense; dependent clauses with time words and *because*

Chapter 6   EMERGENCIES AND STRANGE EXPERIENCES   64

Rhetorical focus: narration
Grammatical and stylistic focus: past continuous tense; time clauses; quotations; the transitional word *then*

Chapter 7   HEALTH AND ILLNESS   74

Rhetorical focus: exposition
Grammatical and stylistic focus: modals *should* and *must;* restrictive
relative clauses; using *in addition, for example,* and *however*

Chapter 8   TELEVISION AND THE MEDIA   90

Rhetorical focus: summarizing a movie plot
Grammatical and stylistic focus: historical present tense; adjectives;
appositives

Chapter 9   FRIENDS AND SOCIAL LIFE   102

Rhetorical focus: biographical narration
Grammatical and stylistic focus: present perfect and present perfect
continuous tenses with *for* and *since;* contrast of verb tenses; using
in fact

Chapter 10   CUSTOMS, CELEBRATIONS, AND HOLIDAYS   116

Rhetorical focus: enumeration
Grammatical and stylistic focus: gerunds and infinitives; using *in
addition to, besides, another,* and *the first, second, third, last;* pronouns;
quantifiers; nonrestrictive relative clauses

Chapter 11   RECREATION   132

Rhetorical focus: persuasion
Grammatical and stylistic focus: present perfect and present perfect continuous tenses; pronouns; gerunds

Chapter 12   YOU, THE CONSUMER   146

Rhetorical focus: writing a formal letter of complaint
Grammatical and stylistic focus: contrast of verb tenses; using past participles as adjectives

          Determining the Characteristics of an Effective Letter of
          Complaint   148

Part II   Developing Writing Skills   150
          Using Past Participles as Adjectives   150
          Using Formal Language   151
          Following the Format of a Business Letter   152

Part III Writing and Editing   156

Part IV   Communicating Through Writing: Answering Letters of
          Complaint   157

          Appendices   159

          Feedback Sheets   165

PREFACE
To the Instructor

INTERACTIONS: THE PROGRAM

Interactions consists of eight texts plus two instructor's manuals for in-college or college-bound nonnative English students. INTERACTIONS I is for high-beginning to low-intermediate students, while INTERACTIONS II is for low-intermediate to intermediate students. Within each level, I and II, the books are carefully coordinated by theme, vocabulary, grammar structure, and, where possible, language functions. A chapter in one book corresponds to and reinforces material taught in the same chapter of the other three books at that level for a truly integrated, four-skills approach.

Each level, I and II, consists of four books plus an instructor's manual. In addition to *A Writing Process Book*, they include:

A Communicative Grammar I, II: Organized around grammatical topics, these books include notional/functional material where appropriate. They present all grammar in context and contain a wide variety of communicative activities.

A Reading Skills Book I, II: The selections in these books are written by the authors and carefully graded in level of difficulty and amount of vocabulary. They include many vocabulary-building exercises and emphasize reading strategies: for example, skimming, scanning, guessing meaning from context, understanding the structure and organization of a selection, increasing reading speed, and interpreting the author's point of view.

A Listening/Speaking Skills Book I, II: These books use lively, natural language from a variety of contexts—dialogues, interviews, lectures, and announcements. Listening strategies emphasized include summarizing main ideas, making inferences, and listening for stressed words, reductions, and intonation. A cassette tape program with instructor's key accompanies each text.

Instructor's Manual I, II: These manuals provide instructions and guidelines for use of the books separately or in any combination to form a program. For each of the core books, there is a separate section with teaching tips and other suggestions. The instructor's manuals also include sample tests.

INTERACTIONS I: A WRITING PROCESS BOOK

Rationale

INTERACTIONS I: A WRITING PROCESS BOOK was designed to lead students through the writing process and provide a variety of activities to help them master the wide array of writing skills necessary for academic writing. The text incorporates a number of features that set it apart from other writing books for nonnative students of English.

While most writing texts concentrate on the end product, giving students little guidance about how to produce it, INTERACTIONS I: A WRITING PROCESS BOOK shows students strategies that they can use in each step of the writing process.

The text consists of twelve chapters, each of which can be used for approximately four to six hours of classroom work. Each chapter is divided into ten sections focusing on different steps in the writing process. These sections introduce various writing strategies and techniques and allow the students to practice them one step at a time. This practice helps the students understand how the different techniques work before they use them in their own writing. Students are given specific guidance in using their new skills to generate and organize ideas and to write, edit, and revise paragraphs of their own. At every step the students are encouraged to analyze and discuss the strategies they are employing. In this way, students focus on one skill at a time. Beginning students especially benefit from this step-by-step approach because they are usually more comfortable with structured practice. By the end of each chapter, the students have acquired new skills and have produced their own paragraphs.

In addition to the twelve chapters, there are appendices at the end of the book to provide spelling, punctuation, and capitalization rules that students can use for reference. There are also feedback sheets for the instructor's use (see Teaching Suggestions).

Although the concept of writing as a process is central to the course, traditional areas of instruction such as paragraph form, mechanics, and grammar are practiced throughout. The emphasis, however, is on those grammatical and lexical features that serve to unify a paragraph.

Our own classroom experience shows that the analysis of model paragraphs can be helpful and instructive. Therefore, the chapters also contain two or three tasks based on model paragraphs.

Chapter Organization

Exploring Ideas: The first problem that most students encounter is a difficulty in generating ideas. This section teaches strategies to help them with this task. Some of the methods presented are discussing and listing ideas, interviewing, and free writing. A vocabulary-building activity provides students with some of the vocabulary they may need in writing their own paragraphs, and encourages them to use fellow students and their teacher as resources for additional vocabulary development.

Organizing Ideas: In this section the students are taught organizational skills such as writing effective topic sentences, limiting the information in a paragraph, and organizing different types of paragraphs.

Developing Cohesion and Style: The focus of this section is on the grammatical and lexical features that serve to unify a paragraph. Students are taught the most natural use of structures and vocabulary in extended written discourse. Some sentence-level structures that often cause students problems, such as choice of tense, are also covered in this section.

Using Correct Form: Each chapter provides practice with the mechanics of writing such as paragraph form, spelling, punctuation, and capitalization.

Writing the First Draft: Because most students do not realize that good writing is usually the product of many revisions, they are explicitly told that the first paragraph they write is only a draft.

Editing Practice: One of the most important skills for students to master is the ability to edit their work. This section provides them with paragraphs that contain common errors of form, grammar, cohesion, and organization. By finding errors in compositions they haven't written, students learn to critically evaluate their work with less anxiety. A positive approach to this step is recommended. Students should not be expected to find all errors, and working in small groups can make this activity more fun.

Editing Your Writing: After students practice editing, they are asked to edit their own compositions. Teachers can ask students to focus on specific aspects of their writing to make this step less frustrating. It is also suggested that students work with partners to help each other with this important step.

Writing the Second Draft: Only after students have had a chance to revise and edit their compositions are they required to hand in neatly written papers for the teacher's evaluation.

Sharing: Too often, students' interest in their writing ends once they receive a grade. This section provides ideas on how students can communicate with each other through their writing. Suggestions include using the writing as the basis of debate or discussion, creating class books with student paragraphs, and displaying writing on bulletin boards.

Using Feedback: This section enables students to use their teacher's feedback to help them evaluate their progress and take responsibility for improving their writing. At the end of the text, feedback sheets are provided. Teachers who wish to focus their feedback on the particular features covered in each chapter will find that these sheets provide an easy method to do so.

Teaching Suggestions

The text has been designed for four hours of classroom per chapter, with homework assignments after each class. Some groups may require more classroom time. Although the text provides a set format, this should not be considered prescriptive. More sophisticated students who may already have developed their own writing strategies should not be forced to abandon them. In addition, we recommend that you ask the students to do as much extra free writing as possible; the instructor's manual contains suggestions for assigning unstructured writing work.

Many tasks in the text are described as pair or group work. Though teachers should consider themselves free to adapt the tasks according to the needs and abilities of their own students, we feel that group and pair work helps students to develop self-confidence. Since writing is such a daunting task for most students, working with others may help them to see that all students have many of the same difficulties.

The feedback sheets at the end of the book are provided to help teachers organize their comments in a way that students can easily interpret. Teachers are encouraged to give as much positive feedback as possible, to focus on content before grammar, and to concentrate on those skills that are presented in each particular chapter. This is especially vital for beginning students, whose mistakes are so numerous.

Acknowledgments

We would like to thank the many people who made these books possible: Mary McVey Gill, our editor, whose ideas, encouragement, and patience were invaluable; Donna Davis, responsible for taking the books through production; Pat Campbell, the copyeditor who smoothed over our rough edges; and Axelle Fortier, the artist, for bringing some of the characters to life. We would also like to thank the many educators who made us aware of the process of writing and the importance of discoursal features—and, finally, our students, the catalysts for all our ideas.

Our thanks also to the following reviewers whose comments, both favorable and critical, were of great value in the development of this text: Janet Anderson, Iowa State University; Lida Baker, University of California, Los Angeles; Marilyn Bernstein, Santa Barbara Community College; Laurie Blass; Sharon Bode, University of Southern California; Phillip Borchers, Arkansas State University; Ellen Broselow, State University of New York, Stony Brook; Joy Durighello, City College of San Francisco; Charles Elerick, University of Texas, El Paso; Jami Ferrer, University of California, Santa Barbara; Anne Hagiwara, Eastern Michigan University; Charles Haynes; Nancy Herzfeld-Pipkin, San Diego State University; Darcy Jack, Los Angeles Unified School District; Patricia Johnson, University of Wisconsin, Green Bay; Debbie Keller, ELS Language Center, Decatur, Georgia; Gail Kellersberger, University of Houston; Elaine Kirn, Santa Monica College; Constance Knop, University of Wisconsin, Madison; James Kohn, San Francisco State University; Lois Locci, De Anza College; Barbara Mallet, College of Mount St. Joseph; Debra Matthews, University of Akron; Beverly McChesney, Stanford University; Sandra McKay, San Francisco State University; Lisa Mets, Vincennes University; Eric Nelson, University of Minnesota, Minneapolis; Helen Polensek, Oregon State University; Virginia Samuda, University of Michigan; Rodney Sciborski, Rio Hondo College; Trish Shannon; Elizabeth Templin, University of Arizona; Ann Thompson, University of Arizona; Mary Thurber, Community College of San Francisco; Richard Van De Moortel; Stephanie Vandrick, University of San Francisco; Patty Werner, University of California, Santa Barbara; Carol Williams, University of California, Riverside; Jean Zukowski-Faust, University of Arizona.

PREFACE
To the Student

Writing is like carrying things up steps. If you try to jump to the top with everything . . .

. . . you will have trouble.

If you carry small armfuls up step by step . . .

. . . you will reach the top.

STEPS TO WRITING

1. Exploring Ideas
2. Organizing Ideas
3. Developing Cohesion and Style
4. Using Correct Form
5. Writing the First Draft
6. Editing Practice
7. Editing Your Writing
8. Writing the Second Draft
9. Sharing
10. Using Feedback

TALKING ABOUT WRITING

Look at the steps to writing.
1. What do you do in each step?
2. Why is each step important?
3. Do you use these steps when you write in your language?

4. Which steps do you like? Why?
5. Which steps do you dislike? Why?

Discuss how you write in your native language with other students in the class. Answer these questions.
1. How many times do you write and rewrite a paper?
2. Do you make an outline?
3. How do you think of ideas?
4. Do you talk with other people about what you write?
5. Do you check your paper for correct grammar, spelling, and punctuation?
6. Do you write in English the same way you write in your language?

Look at this material from papers written by teachers and graduate students.

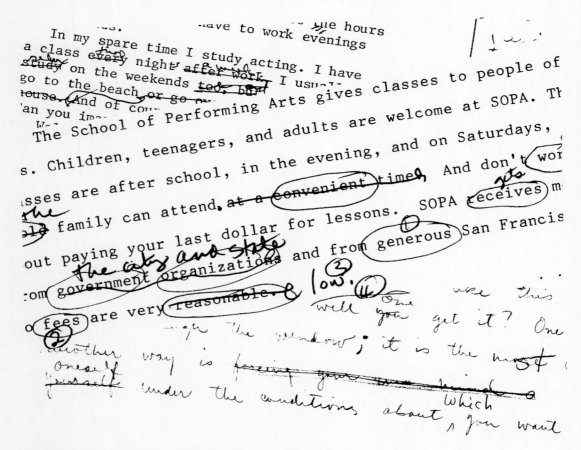

1. Do they write perfect papers the first time?
2. Do they change what they write?
3. Does your writing in your language look like these papers?
4. Now think about the pictures at the beginning of this preface. Why is writing like carrying things up steps?

INTERACTIONS I
A Writing Process Book

1
COLLEGE LIFE

PART I. GETTING READY TO WRITE

Exploring Ideas

A reporter for a college newspaper is writing an article about the new foreign students on campus. She is interviewing some of the students. Look at some of her questions.

1. What is your name?

2. Where are you from?

3. What do you like to do in your free time?

4. What is your occupation?

5. What do you like about the United States?

Interview one of the students in your class for an article for a book about your class. First write some questions. Use some of the questions above and write three other questions. Then your teacher will write some of the students' questions on the board.

Discuss them. Are they good questions to ask? Now look at your questions. Are they good questions to ask? Choose the ten questions you like most. Then choose a partner and interview him or her. Write his or her answers after the questions.

Building Vocabulary

What new vocabulary did you or your partner use? Your teacher will list some of the new words on the board. Discuss the new vocabulary. Use this chart.

Occupations	Free-Time Activities	Majors	Other New Vocabulary
engineer	swim	engineering medical technology	very much
_____	_____	_____	_____
_____	_____	_____	_____
_____	_____	_____	_____
_____	_____	_____	_____

Organizing Ideas

Ordering Information in a Paragraph

The reporter now renumbers her questions in the order she wants to write about. In this kind of paragraph we usually write facts first and then opinions. Look at her new set of questions.

1. What is your name?

2. Where are you from?

3. How old are you?

4. What is your occupation?

5. Why are you in the United States?

6. What do you like about the United States?

7. What do you dislike about the United States?

8. How do you like this college?

9. What do you like to do in your free time?

The reporter interviews a student from Japan. Here are her notes.

1. What is your name? *Yoshi Hiramoto*

2. Where are you from? *Chiba – near Tokyo – seaport*

3. How old are you? *34 years old*

4. What is your occupation? *sales manager*

5. Why are you in the United States? *needs English for job*

6. What do you like about the United States? *likes class, likes American people*

7. What do you dislike about the United States? *doesn't like cafeteria food*

8. How do you like this college? *very much, good*

English class

9. What do you like to do in your free time? *plays tennis, visits sights*

Renumber your questions in the order you want the information to appear in your paragraph. Now write the answers in the correct order. You don't need to write complete sentences. Show your organization to your partner. Does he or she agree with it? Does he or she want to add any information?

Writing Topic Sentences

The topic sentence tells the main idea of the paragraph. You will learn more about topic sentences in other chapters of this book. In your paragraph, the topic sentence introduces your partner and tells something important about him or her. Don't begin paragraphs with *I am going to write about . . .* or *This paragraph is about . . . .* You can begin your paragraph with *(Name of student) is a member of (name of class) at (name of school).* Write your topic sentence here:

_____

_____

PART II. DEVELOPING WRITING SKILLS

Developing Cohesion and Style

Connecting Ideas

Good writers connect the ideas in their paragraphs. A paragraph with connected ideas has *cohesion*. Good writers also use natural English phrases to make a paragraph easy to read. A paragraph with natural English has good *style*.

In this section of the book you will learn how to write paragraphs with cohesion and good style.

1. You will practice verb tenses. A cohesive paragraph has correct verb tenses.

2. You will learn about words such as pronouns that refer to other words in a paragraph.

3. You will learn grammar and vocabulary that improve the style of a paragraph.

4. You will learn special words that connect ideas. In this chapter, you will learn to use *and, but, so,* and *also.*

Look at the reporter's paragraph and circle the words *and, but, so,* and *also.*

International Student at Eastern University

Yoshi Hiramoto is one of 350 international students at Eastern College. He is from Chiba, a seaport near Tokyo. Mr. Hiramoto is 34 years old and is a sales manager for a hospital equipment company. His company sells equipment to American hospitals, so he needs English for his work. Mr. Hiramoto likes the United States very much. He also likes the students in his dormitory. He thinks his English class is excellent, but he thinks the food in the cafeteria is terrible. In his free time Mr. Hiramoto likes to play tennis and visit tourist sights near the university.

Using and *to Connect Phrases*

When you want to say two things about a subject, use the word *and* to connect the verb phrases.

Example: Mr. Hiramoto is 34 years old *and* is a sales manager for a hospital equipment company.

Write sentences from the phrases below. Connect the phrases with *and*.

Example: Klaus is 26 years old and is from Germany.

1. Klaus   is 26 years old   is from Germany

_____

_____

2. Amelia   swims   plays tennis

_____

3. Jorge   is Venezuelan   lives in Maracaibo

_____

4. Reiko   is 19 years old   attends Columbia University

_____

5. Salma   is married   has two children

_____

6. Enrique   likes soccer   plays every Saturday

_____

_____

Using also *to Add Information*

When two sentences give similar ideas, you can use the word *also* in the second sentence. Find the *also* in the reporter's paragraph about Yoshi Hiramoto. *Also* usually goes before the main verb in the sentence, but it goes after the verb *be:*

Example: Mr. Hiramoto likes the United States very much. He *also likes* the students in his dormitory.

Janet is in my English class. She *is also* in a chemistry class.

We use the caret symbol (∧) in corrections to add something to a sentence. Use a ∧ to add *also* to these sentences.

Example: She is very pretty.   She is ∧ very intelligent.
                                            also

1. He likes baseball. He likes rock music.

2. Hamid is tall. He is very athletic.

3. In her free time, Maddie plays basketball. She likes to swim.

4. Efraim works all day. He takes care of his four children.

Now look at your notes from the interview. Write sentences that connect similar information with *and* and *also*. Show your sentences to your partner. Are they correct?

Using and, but, *and* so *to Connect Sentences*

You can connect two sentences with *and*, *but*, or *so*. Use a comma before these words when they connect two complete sentences.

And introduces additional information.

Example: Undergraduates can major in everything from Asian studies to zoology. +

There are many recreational facilities and student services. =

Undergraduates can major in everything from Asian studies to zoology, *and* there are many recreational facilities and student services.

But introduces contrasting information.

Example: He thinks his English class is excellent. +

He thinks the food in the cafeteria is terrible. =

He thinks his English class is excellent, *but* he thinks the food in the cafeteria is terrible.

So introduces a result.

Example: His company sells equipment to American hospitals. +

He needs English for his work. =

His company sells equipment to American hospitals, *so* he needs English for work.

Connect the sentences with *and* or *but*.

1. Alberto lives with his sister. She drives him to school every afternoon.

_____

_____

2. Maria can speak English well. She needs more writing practice.

_____

_____

3. Western University has a beautiful campus. It doesn't have very good library facilities.

_____

_____

4. The college offers a good program in engineering. Its recreational facilities are excellent.

_____

_____

Connect the sentences with *so* or *but*.

1. She has to work all day. She doesn't have time to do all her homework.

_____

_____

2. He likes his English class. He doesn't think the American students are very friendly.

_____

_____

3. Her company is opening an office in the United States. It needs English-speaking workers.

_____

_____

4. She likes campus life. She is homesick for her family.

_____

_____

Look at your notes from the interview and write two or three sentences using *and, but,* and *so* to connect ideas.

_____

_____

_____

_____

_____

_____

_____

Using Correct Form

Following Correct Paragraph Format

Look at the first draft of the reporter's paragraph, which follows. She didn't use good form. Read the rules following the first draft. Then find the reporter's mistakes.

```
international student at eastern university
Yoshi Hiramoto is one of 350 international students at
eastern university. He is from Chiba, a seaport near Tokyo
. Mr. Hiramoto is 34 years old and is a sales manag-
er for a hospital equipment company . his Company sells
equipment to American hospitals, so he needs English for his
work.
Mr. Hiramoto likes the United States very much. he also likes
the students in his dormitory. he thinks his English class is
excellent, but he thinks the food in the cafeteria is
terrible. in his free time Mr. Hiramoto likes to play tenn
is and visit tourist sights near the university.
```

Rules for the Form of Sentences and Paragraphs

1. Write the title in the center of the first line.

2. Capitalize all important words in the title.

3. Don't capitalize small words like *a, the, to, with,* and *at* in titles, except at the beginning of a title.

4. Skip a line between the title and the paragraph.

5. Indent (leave a space) at the beginning of every paragraph.

6. Begin every line except the first at the left margin. (Sometimes a line for the left margin is on the paper. If it isn't, leave a space of one inch.)

7. Leave a one-inch margin on the right.

8. Use a period (.) at the end of every sentence. (For rules on punctuation, see Appendix 3 at the end of this book.)

9. Leave a small space after the period.

10. Begin every sentence with a capital letter. (For rules on capitalization, see Appendix 2.)

11. Also capitalize names of people and places. (See Appendix 2.)

12. If the last word of a line doesn't fit, use a hyphen (-) to break it. You can break a word only between syllables (**e·quip·ment**).

13. Periods and commas (,) must follow words. They can't begin a new line.

14. Every sentence in the paragraph follows the sentence before it. Start on a new line only when you begin a new paragraph.

15. In college writing, most paragraphs have four to ten sentences. A paragraph usually has more than one or two sentences.

Now compare the first draft with this edited paragraph.

International Student at Eastern University

Yoshi Hiramoto is one of 350 international students at Eastern University. He is from Chiba, a seaport near Tokyo. Mr. Hiramoto is 34 years old and is a sales manager for a hospital equipment company. His company sells equipment to American hospitals, so he needs English for his work. Mr. Hiramoto likes the United States very much. He also likes the students in his dormitory. He thinks his English class is excellent, but he thinks the food in the cafeteria is terrible. In his free time Mr. Hiramoto likes to play tennis and visit tourist sights near the university.

Rewrite the following paragraph. Use correct form. When you finish, check it with the rules on pages 10 and 11.

College life at the university of California at berkeley
The University of California at Berkeley has an int
ernational atmosphere, so it is a good place for nonnative
speakers of English to study. it is in the beautiful hills
of a small city near San Francisco and has some of the best
facilities and most famous professors in the United States.
undergraduates at Berkeley can major in eve
rything from Asian studies to zoology, and there are many
recreational facilities and student services. there is a
main library and nine small libraries these libraries have

over 5.6 million books life on this California campus is
usually very informal

  students live in college dormitories and in apartments in
the city of Berkeley, and there are many interesting
activities and events in both Berkeley and San Francisco.

PART III. WRITING AND EDITING

Writing the First Draft

Now write a paragraph about the person you interviewed. Use the topic sentence and
the organization from Section 2 of this chapter. You can also use some of your sentences
with *and, so, but,* and *also.* You don't have to write everything correctly. You can check
it and rewrite it later.

Editing Practice

Edit this paragraph and rewrite it correctly.

A new member joins class
This is about Ana Maria gomez. is a new member
of the English composition class at columbia Community College. There are many classes at columbia .she generally like
her life in the United States.

```
She not likes her apartment.

She is 28 yaers old.

She is from Peru.Ana Maria is married  she have three bea-

utiful children. her children is young she no work right now

 In her free time Ana maria sing and writes songs.
```

Now look at the paragraph carefully. There are many ways to make corrections. Check the paragraph for:

1. Organization
   a. Are all the sentences about one person?
   b. Is the order of the sentences correct?
   c. Does the paragraph have a good topic sentence?

2. Cohesion and style
   a. Can you connect any sentences with *and, so,* or *but*?
   b. Can you add *also* to any sentences?

3. Grammar
   a. Are the verbs correct? Remember that third-person singular verbs end with *-s* in the present tense.
   b. Are the pronouns *he* and *she* correct?

4. Correct form
   a. Does the paragraph have correct form (indentation, capitalization, punctuation, and spelling)? Check the paragraph with the form of the paragraph at the beginning of Section 2.
   b. Is the spelling of all words correct?
   c. Is your handwriting neat?

Discuss your corrections with other students.

Editing Your Writing

Now edit your paragraph. Check it for organization, cohesion, style, form, and grammar. Also check it for content. Is the information in your paragraph true? Is it interesting? Show it to your partner, the person you interviewed. Does he or she want you to add any information? He or she can help you edit your paragraph.

Writing the Second Draft

After you edit your paragraph, rewrite it neatly. Use good handwriting and correct form.

PART IV. COMMUNICATING THROUGH WRITING

Give your paper to your teacher for comments and corrections.

Sharing

Now share your papers with your classmates. Read them aloud or pass them around the room.

Your class can also make a class book with your paragraphs. Students can type or write neat copies of the paragraphs with corrections and your teacher can make copies of them. You can give the book a title and share it with other English classes.

Using Feedback

When your teacher returns your paragraph with comments, look at it carefully. If you don't understand something, ask your teacher about it. The next time you write, look at your teacher's comments. Follow your teacher's instructions and try to correct any mistakes you find.

2 NATURE

PART I. GETTING READY TO WRITE

Exploring Ideas

Look at the picture. Then, in small groups, discuss these questions.

1. What is the title of the painting?

2. Who is Watson?

3. How is the weather? *storming*

4. How many people are there is this picture?

John Singleton Copley, Watson and the Shark, *1778.*

5. How do the men in the boat feel? *afraid, terrified = very afraid.*

6. Is the man in the water afraid?

7. One man is holding something. What is he trying to do? *Kill the shark*

8. What can you see in the background?

9. Is this scene frightening? *yes!*

Building Vocabulary

You are going to write a paragraph describing this scene. Here are some words you may need to write your paragraph. Find out the meaning of any words that you don't understand. Discuss the painting. Complete the chart with new words from your discussion.

Nouns	Adjectives	Verbs	Other
rowboat	huge	reach	_____
shark	frightening	kill	_____
spear	dark	hold	_____
rope	afraid	try	_____
oar	dramatic	attack	_____
background	_____	rescue	_____
ship	_____		_____
teeth	_____		_____
_____	_____	_____	_____
_____	_____	_____	_____
_____	_____	_____	_____

(handwritten: something that makes me feel afraid in fright)
(handwritten: to move toward to get to help. to safe)

Organizing Ideas

Look at this paragraph. It describes the scene in the painting opposite.

This is a picture of a park on a warm and sunny day. It
seems very peaceful. In the park there are many large trees.
On the left you can see a lake with some small sailboats.
There are people in the park. They might be European. Some
people are walking and some are lying or sitting on the
grass. They are wearing old-fashioned clothes. The women are
wearing long dresses and some of them are carrying umbrel-
las. In the middle of the painting there is a small child.
She is walking with her mother. I don't like this painting
very much because the people seem bored.

(handwritten: ~ not modern from the past.)
(handwritten: nothing to do.)

Georges Seurat, Sunday Afternoon on the Island of La Grande Jatte, *1884–1886*.

Ordering Information in a Paragraph

Descriptions often begin with general information and progress to specific points. The first sentence gives a general description. This is the topic sentence. What is the topic sentence in the paragraph about the park? Underline it. Which one of the sentences below is a good topic sentence for a paragraph about *Watson and the Shark*? Circle the number.

1. *Watson and the Shark* is a good painting.

2. In this painting there are some men in a boat.

3. The men in this painting are afraid.

4. This is a painting of a dramatic rescue.

After the writer makes a general statement about the park, he or she gives details. Find the sentences that give details about the park. Then find the sentences that give details about the people.

At the end the writer gives an opinion. Find the sentence that tells you what the writer thinks about the painting.

Here are a student's notes about the picture below, *The Third of May, 1808* by the Spanish painter Francisco Goya. Arrange the notes in order from general to specific. Number them from 1 to 7 (1 is the most general). Put the writer's opinion last. Show your organization to another student. Does he or she agree with it? There may be several correct answers.

a. ___4___ the men are kneeling

b. ___3___ some soldiers are getting ready to shoot some men

c. ___7___ this painting is frightening

d. ___6___ another man is praying

e. ___2___ it is nighttime

f. ___1___ this is a painting of an execution

Francisco Goya, The Third of May, 1808, *1814.*

g. ___5___ one man is holding up his arms

Now make notes for your paragraph about the painting *Watson and the Shark* and organize them.

PART II. DEVELOPING WRITING SKILLS

Developing Cohesion and Style

Adding Details: Adjectives

Adjectives make descriptions more interesting.

   Look at the picture *Watson and the Shark* again. With a partner, make a list of adjectives to describe:

- the boat,
- the weather,
- the man in the water,
- the clothes the men are wearing,
- the shark, and
- the water.

Adjectives can be in two different positions:

1. After the verbs *be, seem,* and *look.*

   Examples: The men are *young.*

   The men look *horrified.*

   NOTE: If you want to use more than one adjective you can connect them with *and*: The shark is huge *and* frightening.

2. Before a noun.

   Example: The *young* men are in a boat.

Add the adjectives from your list to the sentences below.

1. The boat is in the water. _____

_____

2. There is a shark in the water. _____

_____

3. The men are wearing clothes. _____

_____

4. The man in the water seems _____

_____ .

5. The weather looks _____ and _____ .

Adding Details: Prepositional Phrases

Turn back to the paragraph about the Seurat painting of the park. Underline all the phrases that show position (of someone or something). Most phrases that show position begin with prepositions.

Notice that the prepositional phrases can be at the beginning of a sentence or at the end.

> *Examples:*   *In the park* there are many large trees.
> There are people *in the park*.

It is good to put prepositional phrases in different places—not always at the beginning of a sentence, for instance. That way the style of your writing will be interesting.

The sentences opposite describe the painting *The Peasant Wedding*, by Pieter Brueghel. Add one of the prepositional phrases from the list to each sentence. More than one answer is possible.

Pieter Brueghel, Peasant Wedding, *1568.*

in the center

under the table

to the right of center

on the left

on the floor

next to the table

at the table

1. There is a child ___*on the floor*___ .

2. There are two men who are carrying food ___*under the table or next to the table*___ .

3. There is a man who is pouring water ___*on the left*___ .

4. There is a long table ___*in the center*___ ^*standing*^ .

5. There are two musicians ___*next to the table*___ .

6. There are many people ___*at the table*___ ^*sitting*^ .

7. There is a dog ___*under the table*___ .

Using Articles: a/an **and** the

A/an and *the* are articles. They appear before nouns. *A* and *an* are indefinite articles. *The* is a definite article.

Examples: a bicycle   an umbrella   the record   the calendars

A/an and *the* have different uses. Usually *a/an* comes before a noun when the noun appears for the first time. After that, *the* appears before the noun.

Examples: This is *a* painting of *an* island near Paris. *The* island was a popular place to visit during the time of Seurat. *The* painting is very famous.

Complete the sentences with *a/an* or *the*.

1. There is ___*a*___ man on the left. ___*The*___ man is pouring water from ___*a*___ jug.

2. In the center there is ___*a*___ table. ___*The*___ table is very long.

3. Two men are carrying soup on ___*the*___ tray. Another man is serving ___*the*___ soup.

4. There is ___*a*___ child on the floor. ___*The*___ child is holding ___*a*___ bowl.

Using Pronouns

It is very important to use pronouns (words like *I, he, she, it*) when you write a paragraph. Pronouns help to connect your ideas. Underline all the pronouns in the paragraph of the painting of the park. Then draw arrows to connect the pronouns to the nouns they represent.

The paragraph below, about the picture on page 25, seems strange because it doesn't have any pronouns. Change some of the nouns to pronouns. Then compare your new paragraph with a classmate's. Are the changes the same in both?

This is a picture of the members of a family. The family members are having a good time. In the center there is a small girl. The small girl is holding a doll. The small girl likes the doll very much. The children are playing. In the background there is a man. This man is the father. The father is smiling at the children.

Using the Correct Form

Spelling Present Participles Correctly

The present continuous form of the verb has two parts, the verb *be* + the present participle (verb + *-ing*): for instance, *(I) am reading*. Here are some simple spelling rules for adding *-ing* to a verb.

1. If the simple form of the verb ends in a silent *-e* after a consonant, drop the *-e* and add *-ing*.

   Examples: race/racing   move/moving

2. If the simple form ends in *-ie*, change the *-ie* to *y* and add *-ing*.

   Examples: die/dying   untie/untying

3. If the simple form is one syllable and ends in one consonant after one vowel, double the last consonant (except *x*) and add *-ing*.

   Examples: run/running   get/getting

   Note that *w* and *y* at the end of words are vowels, not consonants.

   Examples: row/rowing   play/playing

4. If the simple form ends in a stressed syllable, follow the above rule for one final consonant after one vowel.

   Example: begin/beginning

   If the last syllable is not stressed, just add *-ing*.

   Example: happen/happening

5. In all other cases, add *-ing* to the simple form.

Write the present participles of the following verbs.

Jan Steen, Eve of St. Nicholas, *1666.*

1. write _____   6. study _____
2. sing _____   7. look _____
3. drive _____   8. read _____
4. sit _____   9. see _____
5. stand _____

PART III. WRITING AND EDITING

Writing the First Draft

Now write a paragraph about the painting *Watson and the Shark*. Use your notes. Remember to use the present continuous to tell what's happening. Use *there is* and *there are* to name the things in the painting. Don't worry about mistakes. You can correct them later.

Editing Practice

Edit this paragraph and rewrite it correctly.

```
this is a picture of the hiker. She young. The hiker is

stand on a trail She is wearing the backpack. She wearing

pants long. She is wearing a shirt. She has a walking stick.

In the background you can see some other hikers. I like it

because it is peaceful. The hiker looking into the distance.

She seem happy. Behind her you can see the trees tall. It is

a beautiful scene.
```

Now look at the paragraph carefully. Check it for:

1. Content
   a. Are there interesting adjectives in the paragraph?
   b. Do the adjectives describe the picture well?

2. Organization
   a. Does the paragraph move from the general to the specific?
   b. Do you need to change the order of the sentences?

3. Cohesion and style
   a. Can you connect any sentences?
   b. Are the verbs forms correct?
   c. Do you need to add any adjectives?
   d. Is the use of *a, an,* and *the* correct?

4. Grammar
   a. Is there an *s* on all third-person singular verbs? (The use of the *-s* ending on verbs is *subject-verb agreement.*)
   b. Are the pronouns correct?
   c. Are the adjectives in the correct place?

5. Correct form
   a. Does the paragraph follow the rules for correct form? If you aren't sure, look back at the rules for the form of a paragraph on pages 10–11.
   b. Are the present participles correct?

Discuss your corrections with other students.

Editing Your Writing

Now edit your paragraph. Check it for content, organization, cohesion, style, grammar, and form. Ask your teacher for help if you need it. Then show it to a classmate. Does he or she want you to add or change anything? He or she can help you edit your paragraph.

Writing the Second Draft

Rewrite your paragraph neatly. Use good handwriting and correct form.

PART IV. COMMUNICATING THROUGH WRITING

Give your paragraph to your teacher for comments and corrections.

Sharing

When your teacher returns your paragraph, share it with your classmates. Read it aloud or pass it around the room.

Now you can find another picture and write a paragraph about it. After you edit your new paragraph, you can put the pictures and the paragraphs on a bulletin board.

Using Feedback

Reread your paragraphs from this chapter and Chapter 1. Compare your teacher's comments. Do you see improvement in any area? Which area?

3 LIVING TO EAT OR EATING TO LIVE?

PART I. GETTING READY TO WRITE

Exploring Ideas

Discuss the picture. What are the people doing? What do you think they are eating?

You are going to write a paragraph about the special food you eat for a holiday. First, write about typical everyday meals in your country. Write as much as possible in about five minutes. Don't worry about form or grammar.

Then discuss your paragraph with other students. Make a list of the different kinds of food from the discussion. If you don't know the name of a food, describe it. Maybe your teacher or other students can help you.

POPULAR FOODS

Name	Description
tacos	fried corn pancakes with meat and salad filling

a flatter cake cooked on a skillet

Look at this list of dishes for the American holiday, Thanksgiving. Then think of the food you eat on a holiday in your culture. Make a list of the special dishes next to the Thanksgiving dishes. Sometimes there is no English word for a special dish from your culture. Write the word in your language and explain it.

Holiday: Thanksgiving	*Holiday:* _____ New year
turkey	fish
cranberry sauce	soup

a red, tart, edible berry ① *a liquid dressing for food* ② *stewed fruit*

31

yams inside

put in =   stuffing
        sweet potatoes *(orange inside)*
        pumpkin pie

_____
_____ *sweet* _____
_____ *cake* _____

Remember that some nouns are count nouns—you can count them—and some are not. In small groups, discuss which of your holiday foods on your list are count nouns and which are noncount nouns. Put a check (✔) after the noncount nouns. Some nouns such as *turkey* are sometimes countable and sometimes not. As a meat *turkey* is a noncount noun.

Example: How many *turkeys* are you going to buy? (count)

       Are you going to have *turkey* for Thanksgiving? (noncount)

Now write some sentences that compare the special food you eat on holidays with the food you eat every day.

Example: People usually prepare and eat more food on Thanksgiving. The Thanksgiving meal is more delicious than our everyday meals.

_____
_____
_____
_____
_____
_____
_____

Building Vocabulary

Look at these vocabulary words. Then in small groups look at your classmates' sentences and make a list of words that are new to you. Are the new words nouns, verb phrases, or adjectives?

Nouns	Verb Phrases	Adjectives	Other
celebration	celebrate	joyous	_____
feast	_____	traditional	_____
dish	_____	typical	_____
_____	_____	_____	_____
_____	_____	_____	_____
_____	_____	_____	_____

Organizing Ideas

Ordering Information in a Paragraph

We often begin a paragraph with general ideas and then write more specific ones. The last sentence of a paragraph often describes a personal reaction, opinion, or feeling.

Look at the notes for the Thanksgiving paragraph.

1. Thanksgiving is a family celebration to remember the first harvest of American colonists

2. eat traditional foods from first Thanksgiving feast—many
   foods are Indian

3. eat turkey, stuffing, sweet potatoes, homemade bread, and
   pies

4. eat more food than usual, feel stuffed but happy

Hw
Jan. 5, 90

Now make similar notes for your paragraph. Answer these questions in your notes.

1. What's the name of the holiday? What does it celebrate?
2. Why do people eat special dishes for this holiday?
3. What does your family eat on the holiday?
4. How do you feel about the holiday?

Organize these sentences into the correct order. Number them from 1 for the first in order, to 7, for the last.

1. ___2___7___ Everyone eats more than usual, and at the end of the day we are as stuffed (full) as the turkey.

2. _____4___3___ In my family, everyone brings a special dish for the Thanksgiving meal.

3. _____6_____ My aunt bakes a turkey and fills it with stuffing, a mixture of bread and spices.

4. ___1___1___ Thanksgiving is a family celebration.

5. _____5___4___ They prepare many traditional foods such as turkey, sweet potatoes, and cranberry sauce.

6. ___3___7___ On this day Americans remember the first Thanksgiving feast of the early American colonists.

7. _____6___5___ My relatives also make bread, vegetables, salad, and at least four pies.

Writing Topic Sentences

The topic sentence:

- gives the main idea of the paragraph;
- is always a complete sentence and has a verb;

■ is often the first sentence in a paragraph, but is sometimes the second or even the last sentence.

Which of these main ideas about Thanksgiving are complete sentences? Write a C in front of the complete sentences.

1. _____ C _____ The Thanksgiving meal is a special celebration.

2. _____ I _____ Thanksgiving, an important celebration.

3. _____ C _____ Families eat typical American dishes on Thanksgiving.

4. _____ I _____ A Thanksgiving feast for a family celebration.

5. _____ C _____ Thanksgiving is an ~~important~~ party American holiday.

Which of these sentencs about holidays give main ideas? Write MI in front of those that give main ideas.

T.S. ~ main idea
s.d. supporting detail

1. _____ T.S. _____ The Fourth of July is a celebration of American independence.

2. _____ s.d. _____ We often eat hamburgers on the Fourth of July.

3. _____ s.d. _____ Some people go to church on Christmas morning.

4. _____ T.S. _____ The Christmas meal is an important tradition in Canada.

5. _____ T.S. _____ Easter is a spring celebration.

Look at the sentences about the Thanksgiving meal on page 34. Which sentence is the topic sentence? Now look at your notes and write a topic sentence for your paragraph. It may be the first or the second sentence in your paragraph. Compare your topic sentence with other students' sentences.

PART II. DEVELOPING WRITING SKILLS

Developing Cohesion and Style

Giving Examples with such as

When you write, you can introduce examples with the phrase *such as*. Connect the examples with the word *and*. Do not use the abbreviation *etc.* when you give examples in formal writing.

Example: On Thanksgiving Day we eat many traditional foods. The foods are turkey, sweet potatoes, and cranberries. →
On Thanksgiving Day we eat many traditional foods *such as turkey, sweet potatoes, and cranberries.*

Combine the sentences with the phrase *such as*.

1. On this holiday we eat a lot of fruit. ~~The fruit~~ includes oranges, pineapple, and peaches. _____ *such as* _____
   _____

2. On this day we like to eat many typical Mexican dishes. ~~The dishes are~~ tacos, meat or cheese enchiladas, and tamales. _____ *such as* _____
   _____

3. With the lamb we eat typical Middle Eastern dishes. ~~The dishes are~~ rice, yogurt and cucumbers, and eggplant with sesame sauce. _____ *such as* _____
   _____

4. We fill the dumplings with meat. ~~We use~~ pork, beef, and chicken. _____
   _____ *such as* _____

Look at your list of special foods. Can you use *such as* to give examples of any of the foods? Write a sentence with *such as*. Then compare it with sentences by other students.

_____

_____

Using Appositives

When you talk about typical native dishes, you sometimes have to explain what they are. You can use an *appositive* to explain them. A comma goes before the explanation. A period or another comma goes after the explanation.

Example: My mother fills the turkey with stuffing. Stuffing is a mixture of bread and spices. →
My mother fills the turkey with *stuffing, a mixture of bread and spices.*

Turkey stuffing is a traditional Thanksgiving food. Stuffing is a mixture of bread and spices. →
Turkey *stuffing, a mixture of bread and spices,* is a traditional Thanksgiving food.

Use appositives to combine these sentences.

1. A typical Middle Eastern dish is falafel. ~~Falafel is~~ a mixture of fried chick peas and spices. _____

_____

2. We eat dim sum. ~~Dim sum is~~ a kind of dumpling. _____

_____

3. People like to eat tempura. ~~Tempura is~~ fried shrimp and vegetables. _____

_____

4. A favorite dish is chicken fesenjan. ~~Chicken fesenjan is~~ chicken in a spicy pomegranate sauce. _____

_____

Can you explain any of the typical dishes for your holiday using appositives? Write a sentence with an appositive. Then compare it with sentences by other students.

_____

_____

Using Correct Form

Using Commas with Appositives

Commas separate an appositive from the rest of a sentence.

Examples: On Easter many people make Easter eggs, painted hard-boiled eggs.
        My mother makes Pfefferneusse, a spicy German cookie, for Christmas.

Add commas to these sentences.

1. Rijsttafel, an Indonesian rice and curry dish, is popular in Amsterdam.
2. Americans often eat hot dogs, pork or beef sausages, on the Fourth of July.
3. For breakfast I like to eat blintzes, pancakes with a cheese filling.
4. My friend makes great bouillabaisse, a French fish soup.
5. Spaghetti, an Italian noodle dish, is popular in North America.

Forming Noun Plurals

Write the correct plural forms of these nouns. (See Appendix 1 at the back of this book for spelling rules.)

1. cookie ___cookies___
2. orange ___oranges___
3. peach ___peaches___
4. tomato ___tomatoes___
5. dish ___dishes___

6. pancake ___pancakes___
7. cherry ___cherries___
8. knife ___knives___
9. serving ___servings___

Spelling Third-Person Singular Verbs

Write the correct third-person singular forms of these verbs. (See Appendix 1 for spelling rules.)

1. miss ___misses___
2. watch ___watches___
3. cook ___cooks___
4. eat ___eats___
5. hurry ___hurries___

6. mix ___mixes___
7. play ___plays___
8. wash ___washes___
9. drink ___drinks___

PART III. WRITING AND EDITING

Writing the First Draft

Now write your paragraph. Include the name of the holiday in your title, for example "A Thanksgiving Meal." Use the topic sentence and your notes from Section 2. Try to use *such as* and appositives in your paragraph. What tense will your sentences be in?

Editing Practice

Edit this paragraph and rewrite it correctly.

```
            special christmas foods

Christmas an important holiday for many people in the United

States.

Is the celebration of the birth of Christ. People in North

America prepares many special Christmas foods from all over
```

the the world.Many Christmas specialties fruitcake, eggnog, ham, etc. from Great Britian. North Americans make fruit-cakes with fruits, nuts, and liquors. And eggnog a drink of eggs, milks and rum. I love all the special Christmas food My mother's great-great-grandparents were from Germany. She make German cookie and breads.

Now look at the paragraph carefully. Check it for:

1. **Content**
   a. Is the paragraph interesting?
   b. Is the information clear?

2. **Organization**
   a. Does the topic sentence give the main idea of the paragraph? Is it a complete sentence?
   b. Are all the sentences about the holiday? Are they in a logical order?

3. **Cohesion and style**
   a. Are the appositives correct?
   b. Can you connect any sentences with *and, so,* or *but*?
   c. Does *such as* introduce examples?

4. **Grammar**
   a. Are the present tense verbs correct?
   b. Are the count and noncount nouns correct?

5. **Correct form**
   a. Is the paragraph form (indenting, capitalization, and punctuation) correct?
   b. Is the spelling of words with *-s* endings correct?
   c. Is the use of commas with appositives correct?

Discuss your corrections with other students.

Editing Your Paragraph

Now edit your paragraph. Check it for content, organization, cohesion, style, grammar, and form. Look at your feedback sheets from Chapters 1 and 2. Is there anything you need to check carefully? For example, if your teacher said you need to correct spelling mistakes, check your spelling carefully. Then show your paper to another student. Does he or she understand your paragraph? Does he or she think you need to make any other corrections?

Writing the Second Draft

After you edit your paragraph, rewrite it neatly. Use good handwriting and correct form.

PART IV. COMMUNICATING THROUGH WRITING

Give your paragraph to your teacher for comments.

Sharing

Try to find pictures of the holiday celebration you describe in your paragraph. Bring family pictures or pictures from books to class. In small groups, read your paragraphs aloud and show each other the pictures you have.

Using Feedback

Look at your teacher's comments. If you don't understand something, ask about it. Then make a list of the things you do well and the things you need to work on.

What I do well:

1. _____

   _____

2. _____

   _____

3. _____

_____

What I need to work on:

1. _____

_____

2. _____

_____

3. _____

_____

4 GETTING AROUND THE COMMUNITY

PART I. GETTING READY TO WRITE

Exploring Ideas

A good friend is coming to visit you. You are going to write him or her a letter. In this letter you will tell your friend about some of the things that you might do when he or she comes. First, fill out this chart. Think about the things that your friend might like to do. Think of as many things as you can.

Places to visit:

1. _Graceland_
2. _River_
3. _MSU_
   gymnasium

4. _Peabody Hotel_
5. _Mall of Memphis_
6. _Oak Court Mall_

Things to do:

Inside	Outside
1. _go ice-skating_	1. _go to BB game_
2. _go bowling_	2. _go shopping_
3. _go to a movie_	3. _Play NINTENDo_
go on a picnic	_go dancing_

Compare your list with other students' lists. Are there any things you want to add or change?

In your letter you are also going to give your friend directions to your home. He or she is going to drive to your home.

Look at a map of your town or city. Will your friend have to take a highway? If so, how will he or she get from the highway to your home? Are there any important landmarks to help him or her?

Draw a map that shows the route from the highway to your home. Label all the important streets. Include any important landmarks.

Organizing Ideas

Organizing Paragraphs in a Letter

Your letter will have three paragraphs. Each paragraph has a different purpose. The first one will say hello, discuss the visit, and describe some of the activities you and your friend might do. The second paragraph will give directions to your home. The last paragraph will have only one or two sentences. The purpose of this paragraph is to say good-bye and end the letter.

Look at the sentences below. Decide if they belong in Paragraph 1, 2, or 3. Write 1, 2, or 3 on the line before each sentence. There may be more than one correct answer for each sentence.

43

a. _____1_____ We can also go to a baseball game.

b. _____2_____ There's a gas station on the corner.

c. _____1_____ There's a concert at the City Auditorium.

d. _____2_____ Make a left turn on Maple Avenue.

e. _____3_____ Please write and tell me what time you will arrive.

f. _____2_____ It won't be hard to find my house.

g. _____1_____ It won't be easy to get theater tickets.

h. ____1 or 3____ I'm glad to hear that you are doing well.

i. _____3_____ See you in two weeks.

PART II. DEVELOPING WRITING SKILLS

Developing Cohesion and Style

Using Correct Verb Forms

Complete the sentences with the correct form of the verb in parentheses.

There ___are___ (be) many things to do here. I'm sure that we ___will have___ (have) a good time. It will probably ___be___ (be) hot, so ___bring___ (bring) your bathing suit. There ___is___ (be) a beach very near my home. I ___know___ (know) you like music, and the London Symphony ___will give___ (give) a concert on Saturday night. On Sunday we can ___visit___ (visit) the art museum or go hiking in Butler State Park.

Using Prepositions

Prepositions often show:

1. place
   Example: There's a store on the corner.

2. direction
   Example: Take Highway 6 to Exit 14.

3. distance
   Example: Go straight for two blocks.

Underline the prepositions of place, distance, and direction in the following paragraph. Then exchange papers with another student and compare them.

Take Route 44 south to Exit 12. Turn right at the first light. You will be on Maple

an elementary

Avenue. Go straight down Maple Avenue for two miles. At the corner of Bryant and Maple you will see an elementary school. Turn right at the first street after the school. The name of the street is Roosevelt Drive. Go straight for five blocks. Then make a left turn onto Broadmoor. My apartment building isn't difficult to find. It's on the left, Number 122. You can park your car behind the building.

Now complete the paragraph with the prepositions below.

on

at   on   in   to   for

Turn right _____*at*_____ Smith Drugstore. You will be _____*on*_____ Church Street. Go straight ____*down*____ Church ____*for*____ two blocks. Then turn left ____*at*____ the corner of Church and Findlay. Go straight ____*for*____ one block. Then turn left ____*on*____ Hudson Drive. My house is the third one ____*on*____ the left.

the first one
the second one

Look at the map below. Work with a partner. One student will write directions from the post office to the library. The other student will write directions from the supermarket to the park. Now exchange papers. Can you understand your partner's directions? Make any corrections necessary.

Using **there** *and* **it**   *pronoun ~ words that take the place of a noun.*

Look at these sentences.

> *There* is a supermarket on the corner.
> *It* has a big red and white sign.

The word *it* is a pronoun. It replaces a noun in a sentence. The word *there* does not replace a noun in a sentence. In the sentence above, what noun does *it* replace?

Complete the paragraph with *there* or *it*.

_____*There*_____ are many things to see in Washington. _____*It*_____ is a very interesting city. In the center of the city _____*there*_____ is a large open area. People call _____*it*_____ the mall. All around the mall _____*there*_____ are museums. In the center of the mall _____*there*_____ is a very large structure. _____*It*_____ is the Washington Monument.

Using Correct Form

Writing an Informal Letter

This is a form of an informal letter.

DATE July 12, 1985

SALUTATION

salutation

Dear Bill,

   I am excited about your visit. There's a lot to do here, and I'm sure we'll have a great time. On Saturday afternoon we can go to a basketball game. I think I can get tickets. In the evening we're going to go to Randy's house for dinner. After dinner we might go to a rock concert. I'm going to try to get tickets. If you want, on Sunday we can play tennis in the morning and visit the planetarium in the afternoon.

what to do (future)

   It's easy to find my house. Just take the Connecticut Turnpike east to Exit 5. Turn left at the first light. Then you will be on Bradford Boulevard. Go straight on Bradford for three miles. Then turn left on Apple. You will see a large supermarket on your left. Go to the second light. Make a right turn on Woodgate Road. My building is on the right, three houses from the corner. It's number 417.

(a)

BODY

directions (present)

   See you in two weeks.

Sincerely,

CLOSING

Steve

good-bye

DATE: The date usually appears so that it ends at the right margin. The order of the date is month, day, year. Capitalize the name of the month and put a comma after the day and before the year. Do not use a comma in the year.

April 4, 1983

SALUTATION: Most letters begin with *Dear*. Use the name that you usually call the person. In an informal letter a comma goes after the name.

> Dear Professor Hudson,
> Dear Dr. Fitzgerald,
> Dear Mr. and Mrs. White,
> Dear Melinda,

BODY: Indent each paragraph of the letter. In letters, paragraphs may have only one or two sentences. Although it is important to keep each paragraph on the same topic, the paragraphs in a letter do not always begin with a topic sentence.

CLOSING: The closing of a letter begins either at the left or in the center of the page. There are many different closings. The closing that you choose depends on your relationship with the person you are writing to.

> Regards,   used for informal letters
>
> Fondly,   used only for close friends or
> Love,   relatives

Addressing an Envelope

This is the correct way to address an envelope.

```
Carol Martin                                          STAMP
128 Lake Drive, Apt. 8     RETURN ADDRESS
Muskegon, Michigan 49441
              ZIP CODE



                   Mr. and Mrs. Daniel Kaufman

       ADDRESS     432 St. George St.

                   Toronto, Canada M56 2V8

                             POSTAL CODE
```

RETURN ADDRESS: Write your address in the top left-hand corner of the envelope.

ADDRESS: Write the address clearly. You may want to print it. Make sure the address is complete. If there is an apartment number, be sure to include it. It is also important to use the zip code or postal code.

PART III. WRITING AND EDITING

Writing the First Draft

Now write your letter to your friend. Then address an envelope.

Editing Practice

Edit this letter and rewrite it correctly.

june 15, 1986

dear Mary I'm very glad that you will visit me next week. We will

to have a good time. It's easy to find my house. Make a left

turn near the corner of Broadway and Fifth Street. Drive
down Fifth to two blocks. Make a right turn in Henry Street.
It is a park on the corner. My house is in the left side. It
are number 150. The weather is cold so we might going ski.
We can go skating. Please to bring your photo album. I want
see the pictures of your family. Sally

Now look at the letter carefully. Check it for:

1. Content
   a. Are the activities interesting?
   b. Are the directions clear?

2. Organization
   a. Is each paragraph about a different topic?
   b. Is there a salutation and closing?

3. Cohesion and style
   a. Are the verb tenses correct?
   b. Are the prepositions correct?
   c. Is the use of *there* and *it* correct?

4. Grammar
   a. Are the verb forms correct?
   b. Is there an *s* on third-person singular verbs in the present tense?

5. Correct form
   a. Is the date correct?
   b. Is the salutation correct?
   c. Do the paragraphs begin with an indentation?
   d. Is the closing in the right place?

Discuss your corrections with other students.

Editing Your Writing

Now edit your letter. Check it for content, organization, cohesion, style, grammar, and form. Exchange letters with another student and talk about them.

Writing the Second Draft

After you edit your letter, rewrite it neatly. Use good handwriting and correct form.

PART IV. COMMUNICATING THROUGH WRITING

Give your letter to your teacher for comments.

Sharing

Show your letter to another student. Can he or she understand your directions? He or she can try to draw a map from the highway to your house using your directions.

Using Feedback

Look at your teacher's comments. If you don't understand something, ask about it. Do you see improvement in any area of your writing?

5 HOUSING AND THE FAMILY

PART I. GETTING READY TO WRITE

Exploring Ideas

In this chapter you are going to write about a part of your life. You can make a lifeline to help you. This is a line that shows the important events of your life.

    First draw a line down the middle of a piece of paper. The top of the line represents the year you were born, and the bottom of the line is the present time. You can write some ages along the line too, as in the example.

Now relax and think about your life. Think in English, if possible, and also think in pictures. As you think, try to answer these questions:

1. What important things happened to me?

2. What important decisions did I make?

3. Who were the important people in my life?

4. How did I feel at different times in my life?

5. What were the important changes in my life?

After you think about your life, write some of the important events on the left of the lifeline and feelings about your life on the right. Write in English if possible, but don't worry about correctness or order. If you can't think of something in English, use your native language. You can use pictures and symbols, and you may also want to look at family photographs. Here is an example of Greta's lifeline and some photos from her life.

Lifeline

Events   < 0   ## Feelings

Was a twin in a large family

- Always felt secure,
- always had a friend,
- was scared of strangers

Went to school, different class from twin   < 5

- Separation was difficult but grew to like school

- Not very much happened in childhood

< 10 - Liked to read, ski

- Became a teenager, skied a lot

- was shy, not popular
- skiing gave me confidence

When I was sixteen I taught skiing at a resort on weekends   < 15

Enjoyed my job, became less shy

- Graduated from secondary school

Came to States to study English

< 20

Now show your lifeline to some other students and talk about your life. Ask each other questions. What do the other students think is interesting about your life?

Building Vocabulary

These new words are in the sample lifeline. Discuss their meanings and then add words that you and other students used.

Nouns	Verbs	Adjectives	Other
twin	was born	popular	_____
self-confidence	grew up	scared	_____
childhood	_____	shy	_____
_____	_____	_____	_____
_____	_____	_____	_____
_____	_____	_____	_____

Did you need to write any words or phrases in your native language? Look them up in a dictionary and write their meanings in English. Then write a sentence that uses each new word or phrase. Also write sentences with English words you're not sure how to use. Show your sentences to the other students in your group. Do they think you used the words correctly? Then your teacher will check your sentences.

Organizing Ideas

Limiting Information

You can't write about your whole life in one paragraph, so you need to choose one part of your life to write about. You may want to write about your childhood, your school years, or one important event in your life. Look at the lifeline of the twin and discuss where a paragraph on a part of a life can begin and end.

Now look at your lifeline and decide what part of your life you want to write about. Draw lines to show where your paragraph can begin and end. Discuss your decision with other students. Answer these questions to help you decide what part of your life to write about.

1. Is the part you chose interesting? You may want to write about unusual or funny events in your life because they are more interesting.

2. Is the part you chose important? Because you can't write your whole life story in one paragraph, choose one important event or time.

3. Is the part you chose all about one topic? Don't choose many different events or times. Everything in your paragraph should be on one subject.

Making Paragraph Notes

Look at the part of the lifeline you chose and add information you think is important.
Cross out information that is not about the topic of your paragraph.

Writing Topic Sentences

Look at these paragraph notes. For each paragraph, circle the topic sentence that you
think gives the main idea. Discuss your choices with your classmates.

Paragraph 1

- ```
  was born a twin—-very important to childhood
  ```
- ```
  large family
  ```
- ```
  always had a friend, felt secure
  ```
- ```
  went to school and was in different classes from twin
  ```

Topic sentences:

1. Because I was born a twin, I had a very different childhood from most people.
2. Because I had a twin, I felt secure.
3. I didn't like school because I was in different classes from my twin.

Paragraph 2

- ```
  teenage years difficult
  ```
- ```
  liked to read, was shy, not popular
  ```
- ```
  was a good skier
  ```
- ```
  taught skiing at a resort
  ```
- ```
  this gave me self-confidence
  ```

Topic sentences:

1. I wasn't popular as a teenager.
2. As a teenager, I taught skiing at a ski resort.
3. My teenage years were very difficult at first, but they ended happily.

Now write a topic sentence that gives the main idea for your paragraph. Show the notes
  ```

for your paragraph and your topic sentence to other students. Do they think you need to change anything?

_____

_____

Writing Titles

The title should give the main idea of a composition. It should also be interesting. It goes on the top line of the paper and is not a complete sentence. Look at the possible titles for the paragraphs about the twin. Put a checkmark by the titles that you like. Why do you like them?

Paragraph 1

My Childhood   Difficult School Years
Born a Twin   My Childhood as a Twin

Paragraph 2

Growing Up   Teenage Years
Unhappy Teens   Life at a Ski Resort

Now look at your paragraph notes and write a title for your paragraph.

PART II. DEVELOPING WRITING SKILLS

Developing Cohesion and Style

Using the Past Tense

Because you are writing about events in the past, most of your sentences will be in the past tense. Complete the following paragraph with the correct past-tense forms of the verbs in parentheses. For the spelling of verbs with *-ed*, see Appendix 1 at the back of this book.

Because I _____*was*_____ (be) born a twin, I _____*had*_____ (have) a very different childhood from most people. There _____*was*_____ (be) always someone to play with and I always _____*had*_____ (have) a friend. My mother said we _____*fed*_____ (feed) each other, _____*played*_____ (play) together, and _____*cried*_____ (cry) when strangers came near. We _____*did*_____ (do) everything together. When my sister _____*needed*_____ (need) special shoes, I _____*wanted*_____ (want) them too. But life as a twin _____*wasn't*_____ (not be) always great. My mother _____*didn't have*_____ (not have) enough milk for both of us, and the one she didn't nurse _____*was*_____ (be) always sick. My father ___*said*___ (say) he ___*hated*___ (hate) to come home because

with my older brother there ___*were*___ (be) three screaming babies in the house.

Even now I think that when I get something I want, someone else will go without.

Now look at your paragraph notes and make a list of the past-tense verbs you might use. Compare your list with those of other students. Can you use any of their words? Also be careful to use past-tense verbs only for completed events. You can't write "I went to school for three years" if you are still going to school.

Combining Sentences with Time Words and because

When you write a paragraph that describes events, you can use these time words to combine sentences:

before	when
after	as soon as

You can also combine sentences with *because* to show reasons. To review how to combine sentences with *and*, *but* or *so*, see Chapter 1.

Complete the following paragraph with *before, after, when, because, and, but,* or *so*.

I had a typical childhood, ___*but*___ my life changed ___*when*___ I was

fourteen. We moved from our small village to Karachi, a big city in Pakistan.

(When)· ___*After*___ we moved, I became shy and nervous. The other boys in my classes

were tough, ___*and*___ they laughed at my country ways. ___*Because*___ I

didn't like the other boys, I became more interested in books. I always liked biology,

___*so*___ I started to read about medicine. I was very unhappy at the time,

___*but*___ I'm glad this happened ___*because*___ I finally decided to become a

doctor.

Finish these sentences. Use information about your life if you can.

1. When I became a teenager, I ___*started to help my mother.*___
_____ .

2. I came to the United States because ___*I wanted to countine*___
___*my education.*___ _____ .

3. When I was a child, I ___*easily cried.*___ _____
_____ .

4. After I left high school, I _entered the Chung Chy University._

5. Before I started this class, I _did my homework._

6. I wasn't very happy, but _I was patient._
, but I had friends who were always with me.

Now write at least two sentences about your life, using the information in your paragraph notes. Use *because, before, after,* or *when.*

Because they come, I can't go.
Before
After
When

Using Correct Form

Capitalizing Titles

In the title, capitalize the first word and all the important words. Do not capitalize the following kinds of words (unless they are the first word in the title):

1. conjunctions: *and, but, or, so*

2. articles: *the, a, an*

3. short prepositions: *at, by, for, in, of, on, out, to, up, with*

Write these titles with the correct capitalization.

1. an exciting life _An Exciting Life_

2. all's well that ends well _All's Well That Ends Well_

3. a gift of hope _A Gift of Hope._

4. the best years of my life _The Best Years of My Life_

5. going away _Going Away_

6. a happy ending _A Happy Ending_

7. life in a new city _Life in a New City_

8. best friends ___Best Friends___

9. a new beginning ___A new beginning___

10. a wonderful experience ___A wonderful Experience.___

Punctuating Compound Sentences

When you use *and, but, so,* and *or* to combine sentences, a comma generally goes before the conjunction. Don't use a comma if the conjunction doesn't combine sentences.

Examples: My brother was ten at the time, and I was twelve.
We went to school in the morning and played all afternoon.

Add commas to these sentences if the conjunction combines two complete sentences.

1. We didn't have very much money, so we moved into my aunt's house.

2. I was happier and prouder than ever before.

3. We moved to Texas and lived with my brother's family.

4. I was happy to get the scholarship, but I didn't want to leave my family.

5. My grandmother was the most important person in my life, and I was very unhappy when she died.

Punctuating Sentences with Dependent Clauses

Clauses beginning with time words (like *when, before*) or *because* are not complete sentences—they are dependent clauses. You must combine them with an independent clause—a clause that is a complete sentence by itself. If you don't combine them with an independent clause, they are sentence fragments. If the dependent clause appears at the beginning of a sentence, use a comma after it. If the dependent clause appears at the end of the sentence, don't use a comma in front of it.

Examples: When I was five, we moved to Caracas.
We moved to Caracas when I was five.
Because my father had a new job, we moved to Caracas.
We moved to Caracas because my father had a new job.
Sentence fragment: We moved to Caracas. Because my father had a new job.

Some of these sentences have correct punctuation and some don't. Write *correct* after the sentence if the punctuation is correct. Rewrite the sentences with correct punctuation if it is wrong.

1. *Before* we moved here, we used to have many friends and relatives nearby. _____

_____

_____

2. *Because* my uncle was an engineer, he sent me to engineering school. _____
_____

3. I left the farm, *as soon as* I could. _____
_____

4. We moved to Colorado, *Because* the doctors said I needed a dry climate. _____
_____

5. *When* I first came here, I loved the excitement of New York. _____
_____

6. I came to the city, *when* I was five. _____
_____

cancel the ,

PART III. WRITING AND EDITING

Writing the First Draft

Now write your paragraph about a part of your life. Use the topic sentence and the notes you made in Section 2. Also combine some sentences with time words and *because, and, but,* and *so*. Remember to use the past tense when you write about completed actions.

Editing Practice

Edit this paragraph and rewrite it correctly.

fallen
fell   *How*

                    how I Became a jazz Musician
                                              was
I fall in love with jazz, When I have five years. I always

heared jazz in the streets, but for my fifth birthday my

brother tooks me to a concert. Their I saw great saxophonist
                                  There
and decided to learn to play the saxophone. First I need *a*

saxophone, So I ask my father. My father he say he no have

money for a saxophone. I work for my brother, uncles, ~~and~~
cosins. I made a little money. Then my father ~~he~~ see I
work hard. My father is bus driver. He give me money for
saxophone. I listen to albums. And my brother ~~he~~ teach me. I
practice every day. Soon I am saxophone player good.

Now look at the paragraph carefully. Check it for:

1. Content
   a. Is the information interesting?
   b. Is the information important?

2. Organization
   a. Does the topic sentence give the main idea of the paragraph?
   b. Are all of the sentences about one topic?
   c. Should you change the order of any of the sentences?

3. Cohesion and style
   a. Did you use the correct past tense verbs?
   b. Did you combine sentences with time words and *and, but,* or *so*?

4. Grammar
   a. Are your nouns, pronouns, and articles correct?
   b. Did you use good sentence structure (no sentence fragments)?

5. Correct form
   a. Did you use correct paragraph form?
   b. Did you capitalize the words in the title correctly?
   c. Did you use correct punctuation when you combined sentences?
   d. Did you spell the words correctly?

Discuss your corrections with other students.

Editing Your Writing

Now edit the paragraph you wrote. Check it for content, organization, cohesion, style, grammar, and form. Exchange paragraphs with another student and talk about them.

Writing the Second Draft

After you edit your paragraph, rewrite it neatly. Use good handwriting and correct form.

PART IV. COMMUNICATING THROUGH WRITING

Give your paragraph to your teacher for comments.

Sharing

Let other students read your paragraph. You may want to show them pictures of you and your family, too. Discuss the experiences you wrote about. Did other students have similar experiences? Do you have questions about the other students' paragraphs?

Using Feedback

Look at your teacher's comments. If you don't understand something, ask about it. Then look at all the paragraphs you wrote with your teacher's comments and make a list of goals. Write down things you can do to improve your writing. Use these questions to help you write your goals.

1. Are your paragraphs interesting?

2. Are your ideas clear?

3. Are you organizing your paragraphs well?

4. Are you using good topic sentences?

5. Are there any grammatical structures you need to practice?

6. Do you need to use neater handwriting?

7. Is your spelling correct?

8. Are you using correct paragraph form?

9. How is your punctuation and capitalization?

10. Are you trying to write sentences that are too difficult?

6 EMERGENCIES AND STRANGE EXPERIENCES

PART I. GETTING READY TO WRITE

Exploring Ideas

Read this story.

It was a day just like any other day. Marvin got up when his alarm clock rang at seven o'clock. He smiled as he put on his uniform. Then he stood up straight and looked at himself in the mirror. He saw a short, slightly overweight man with a small moustache and a kind face. "At least the uniform looks good," he thought. He liked the blue uniform. When he put it on, he felt important.

Marvin listened to the news while he made breakfast in his tiny kitchen. The announcer was saying something about an escaped convict, but Marvin wasn't paying attention. He was thinking about his father. His

neat – likes everything clean *dependable*

punctual

father was disappointed with him. Marvin knew that. But it wasn't his fault that he was too short to be a police officer.

After he finished his breakfast, Marvin prepared to leave for work. He washed his breakfast dishes, watered his plants, and fed his cat, Amelia. He arrived at work exactly on time. He always did.

There was a lot of mail that day. Before he could make his deliveries, he had to sort the letters and packages. When he finished, he put the mail into his large brown bag, put the bag on his shoulder, and left the post office.

One of his first stops was Dr. Jordan's house. As he was putting the mail into the mailbox, he heard a noise inside the house. "That's strange," he thought. "The Jordans are on vacation. They won't be home until tomorrow." He decided to go and look in the window.

In this chapter you are going to write the ending to this story. Before you write you should think about Marvin.

65

Look at these pictures. Which one do you think looks like Marvin?

Now think about Marvin's personality. Answer these questions and give reasons for your answers.

1. Is he lonely? _____ Yes, he is lonely. _____

_____

2. Is he confident? _____ no, _____

_____

3. Is he happy? _____ no, _____

_____

4. Is he neat? _____ yes. _____

_____

5. Is he responsible? _____ yes. _____

_____

6. Does he work hard? _____ yes. _____

_____

7. What can you tell about Marvin from his apartment? _____

_____

Now think about an ending for the story. Use these questions as a guide.

1. What did Marvin see when he looked in the window?

2. What did he decide to do after he looked in the window?

3. Why did he decide to do this?

4. How did he feel?

Make notes for your ending, but do not write it yet.

Building Vocabulary

Ask the teacher about any vocabulary words that you need. Add the new vocabulary to this list.

Nouns	Verbs	Adjectives and Adverbs	Other
murderer	hit	strong	_____
gun	shoot	frightened	_____
convict	arrest	_____	_____
safe	steal	_____	_____
_____	break in	_____	_____
_____	*theif*	_____	_____
_____	*burglar*	_____	_____
_____	_____	_____	_____

You will have to write your ending in the past tense. Do you know the past forms of all the verbs you want to use?

Organizing Ideas

Using a Time Sequence

Writers use time words such as *before, after, as, when, while, then,* and *as soon as* to organize the information in a story. Look at the story again. Make a list of the time words. Compare your list with another student's. Are there any words you missed?

Limiting Information

You must write your ending in one paragraph. The paragraph should have 100 to 150 words. It is important to limit what you want to say.

Look at your notes. Tell your story to another student. With that student discuss these questions:

1. Is my ending too complicated?

2. Did I include too much description?

3. Can I fit everything into one paragraph?

Writing a Title

The title of a story should be interesting and not too general, but it should not tell the reader how the story will end. Which of these do you think is a good title? Circle the number. Why do you think it's good?

1. Marvin Runs Away
2. The Murder of Marvin
3. A Big Day for a Little Man
4. Marvin Catches a Thief
5. Marvin the Mailman

Now give your story a title. You may use one of these or make up your own.

PART II. DEVELOPING WRITING SKILLS

Developing Cohesion and Style

Using when, while, *and as* with the Past Continuous and the Simple Past Tenses

If you want to talk about two actions in the past and one action interrupts the other, use *when* to introduce the interrupting action.

Example: The robber was opening the safe *when* the police officer came in.

Use *while* or *as* to introduce the action in progress, the action that *was happening*.

Examples: *While* the robber was opening the safe, the police officer came in.
As the robber was opening the safe, the police officer came in.

Use *while* or *as* when the two actions happen at the same time.

Examples: One robber was opening the safe while the other one was watching for the police.
Marvin listened to the radio as he ate breakfast.

Use *when* if one action follows the other.

Example: *When* the police officer entered the house, he heard a noise.

Combine these sentences with *when, while,* or *as.* More than one answer may be correct.

1. Marvin was looking in the window. Someone grabbed his arm. _____
   _____While_____ , someone

2. The man grabbed his arm. Marvin started to fight. _____
   (as)
   _____When_____ , marvin started to fight.

3. A neighbor saw the fight. He called the police. _____
   _____When a_____ , he
   arm

4. One robber was in the house stealing the jewelry. Marvin and the other robber were fighting. _While one_ _____, _Marvin_ _____ .

_____

5. Dr. Jordan gave Marvin a reward. He heard the story. _____

__ _Dr. Jordan_ _____ _when he heard_ _____

Look at the notes for your story and write three sentences: one with *when*, one with *while*, and one with *as.* _____

_____

_____

_____

_____

_____

_____

Using as soon as

As soon as is similar to *when*.

Examples: *As soon as* he saw the thief, he ran away.

He ran away *as soon as* he saw the thief.

However, *as soon as* emphasizes that one action happened *immediately* after another.

Combine these sentences with *as soon as.* For each pair of sentences decide if *as soon as* goes at the beginning or in the middle of the sentence.

1. The thief saw Marvin. He started to run. _____

As soon as the thief saw marvin, he started to run.

2. Marvin called an ambulance. He saw Dr. Jordan. _____

Marvin _____ _as soon as he saw Dr. Jordan._

3. The police arrived. They arrested Marvin. _____

As soon as the police ——, they ————

4. The neighbor ran outside. He heard the shot. _____

The _____ _as soon as he heard the shot._

Using then

You can use *then* when you are narrating a story. By using *then*, you can make the time sequence clear and not repeat the same words. Compare:

Examples: I ran out of the house. After I ran out of the house, I saw a man in the street.

I ran out of the house. Then I saw a man in the street.

Varying Time Words and Phrases

Now you have learned several different time words:

when   *while*   *before*   *after*   *then*   *as soon as*

Although these words do not have exactly the same meaning, you can use some of them in place of others.

Examples: *When* he saw the thief, he called the police.
He called the police *as soon as* he saw the thief.

After he saw the thief, he called the police.
He saw the thief. *Then* he called the police.
He saw the thief *before* he called the police.

To make your writing more interesting, it is important to vary the words you use. Complete the sentences with the time words listed above.

Marvin put down his mailbag. _____Then_____ he tiptoed over to the window.

_____While_____ he looked inside he saw a man's shadow. _____Then_____ he

had to make a decision. Should he call the police or should he go into the house?

_____While_____ he was thinking, Marvin heard two voices from inside the house.

There were *two* men! _____When_____ he realized this, he knew he couldn't go into

the house alone, and he decided to go call the police. _____Before_____ he could leave

the window, he felt a hand on his arm.

Using Descriptive Words   *adj. adv.*

An interesting story tells the reader more than just what happened. It also describes important people or places. Underline the descriptive words and phrases in the story about Marvin. Then look at the notes for your paragraph. Add adjectives that describe the people and places.

Using Quotations

A good story also tells the reader what the characters are thinking. In the story about Marvin, the writer used quotations to show what Marvin was thinking. Underline the sentences that tell you about Marvin's thoughts. Look at the notes for your paragraph again. Write down some of Marvin's thoughts that you will include.

When you write exactly what someone said or thought, you use quotation marks. Use quotation marks in pairs. Use one set at the beginning of the quotation and one at the end.

Examples: "He looks like a thief!" Marvin thought.
             Marvin thought, "He looks like a thief!"

A quotation is always set off from the rest of the sentence by a comma, a question mark, or an exclamation point.

Examples: "I should call the police," Marvin thought.
             "Maybe," Marvin thought, "I should call the police."
             "Stop those men!" Marvin yelled.
             "Should I try to stop them?" Marvin asked himself.

Look at these sentences. Put quotation marks in the correct places.

1. Marvin thought, Who are those men?

2. You should be a policeman, Marvin's father said.

3. Come out of there! Marvin yelled.

4. Do you have a gun? Marvin asked.

Now look at the quotations you wrote for your ending and add quotation marks.

PART III. WRITING AND EDITING

Writing the First Draft

Now write your ending to the story about Marvin. Remember to:

1. use time words where they are necessary

2. include descriptive words

3. use quotations

Editing Practice

Edit this paragraph and rewrite it correctly. It is a possible ending to the story.

```
   Marvin saw a man, while he looked in the window. As soon

as he decided to go inside. He walk around to the back door.

Before he opened the door. He looked in the back window.

Then he thought maybe the man had a gun. Marvin decided to

call the police. Suddenly he heard a woman scream. ''There's

a man looking in the kitchen window! Before Marvin heard the

voice he knew the answer to the mystery! Dr. Jordan and his

family were home.
```

Now look at the paragraph carefully. Check it for:

1. Content
   a. Is the story clear?
   b. Is all the information important?

2. Organization
   a. Did you use time words where necessary?
   b. Did you add a title?

3. Cohesion and style
   a. Did you vary the time words and expressions?
   b. Did you include enough description?
   c. Did you use quotations?

4. Grammar
   a. Did you use the correct form of the past tense?
   b. Did you use the correct form of the present continuous tense?
   c. Did you use good sentence structure?

5. Correct form
   a. Did you use commas correctly?
   b. Did you use quotation marks correctly?

Discuss your corrections with other students.

Editing Your Writing

Now edit the paragraph you wrote. Check it for content, organization, cohesion, style, grammar, and form. Exchange paragraphs with another student and talk about them.

Writing the Second Draft

After you edit your paragraph, rewrite it neatly. Use good handwriting and correct form.

PART IV. COMMUNICATING THROUGH WRITING

Give your paragraph to your teacher for comments.

Sharing

Read your ending to the other students in the class.

Using Feedback

Look at your teacher's comments. If you don't understand something, ask about it. There are some common editing symbols that your teacher may use. In Chapter 1 you learned about the caret (∧).

Example: ∧ The Thief ran out the door.

Here are some others:

sp = wrong spelling   = take out this word or punctuation
sf = sentence fragment   O = add punctuation here

Now rewrite these sentences.

1. The police oficer helped Marvin. _The police officer helped Marvin._
_____

2. Then he went to the police station. _____
_____

3. When he arrived there, He saw Dr. Jordan. _____
_____

4. While he was talking to the doctor Marvin came in. _____
_____

5. Marvin's father very proud of him. _____
_____

CHAPTER

7
HEALTH AND ILLNESS

PART I. GETTING READY TO WRITE

Exploring Ideas

Look at these pictures and discuss them. What kinds of treatments are the people using? What do you think of these treatments?

Now discuss these questions in small groups.

1. What do people in your culture do when they have colds? Do they usually take modern medicines? What traditional treatments do they use?

2. What do you do when you have a cold? Do you think modern treatments or traditional treatments are better?

3. What other traditional treatments do people in your culture use? What do you think of them? Do the people in your group know about any similar treatments?

Building Vocabulary

Add new words or expressions you used in your discussion to this list.

acupuncture   herbal medicine

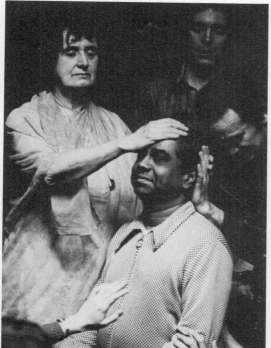
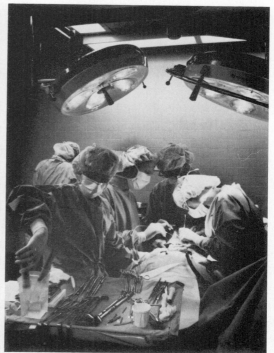

Faith healing   surgery (operation)

(religion - people put their hands on you and pray)

Nouns	Verbs	Adjectives	Other
treatment	treat	psychic	_____
acupuncture	heal	_____	_____
needles	take (medicine)	_____	_____
midwife	massage	_____	_____
healer	_____	_____	_____
herbal	_____	_____	_____
Faith	_____	_____	_____
healing	_____	_____	_____
surgery	_____	_____	_____

Organizing Ideas

Making an Idea Map

You are going to write a paragraph about traditional treatments that people in your culture sometimes use. To get your ideas on paper, make an "idea map." Write the words *traditional treatments* in the middle of a piece of paper. Then write all your ideas about that topic around the paper. Connect the ideas that go together. Look at this example of an idea map of traditional treatments popular in the United States and Canada.

Look at your idea map and make a list of the ideas you think would make a good paragraph. Use these questions to help you decide.

1. Is the information interesting?

2. Do you have enough information for a paragraph?

3. Can you limit the information to a single paragraph?

4. How do you want to organize your information?
    a. the different ways people use one kind of treatment
    b. the different treatments people use for one illness
    c. a short description of several different treatments you are familiar with

Writing Topic Sentences

Circle the letter of the best answer.

1. Choose the best topic sentence for a paragraph about herbs.
    a. People often make teas with herbs to cure sore throats.
    b. People in my country use herbs to treat many different diseases.
    c. I don't think herbs are as good as modern medicines.

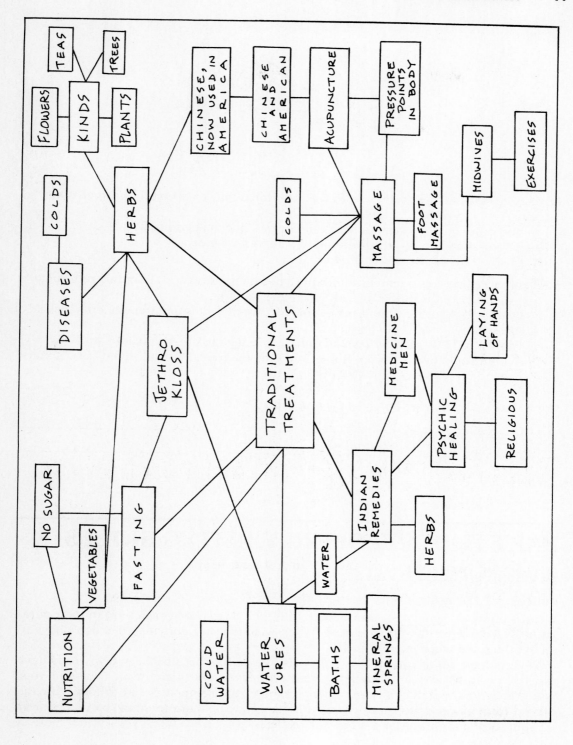

2. Choose the best topic sentence for a paragraph about traditional treatments for colds.
   a. You don't have to spend a lot of money at a pharmacy to treat a cold.
   b. Lemon juice is a good traditional treatment for colds.
   c. I had a horrible cold a year ago.

3. Choose the best topic sentence for a paragraph about several different traditional treatments popular in the United States and Canada.
   a. One traditional treatment people in the United States and Canada often use is massage.
   b. People in the United States and Canada often go to nutritionists.
   c. Many people in the United States and Canada are using traditional treatments instead of modern medicine to treat a variety of health problems.

Now write a topic sentence for your paragraph.

a person who tells you what food to eat

_____

_____

PART II. DEVELOPING WRITING SKILLS

Developing Cohesion and Style

Unifying a Paragraph with Synonyms

Writers often use synonyms (words with the same or a similar meaning) in their paragraphs. Synonyms unify a paragraph. When writers use synonyms, they don't have to repeat the same word many times.

Writers have to be careful when they use synonyms because very few words have exactly the same meaning. Look at these synonyms you might want to use in your paragraph. Read the definitions. Then complete the sentences that follow with the correct form of an appropriate synonym. There may be more than one correct answer for some of the sentences.

Nouns

treatment = anything people use to try to cure a disease or improve health
cure = a medicine or treatment to make a disease go away
remedy = a medicine or treatment that cures a disease
medicine (usually noncount) = (1) the science of health; (2) a drug a person takes to get
   over a sickness

1. When I have a cold, I take _____*medicine*_____ three times a day.

2. I had several acupuncture _____*treatment*_____ , but I did not get better.

3. Scientists don't have any _____*cure*_____ for cancer.

4. The best _____*remedy*_____ for a cold is rest, even though doctors have no single
   (n)
   cure.

Symptom — how you feel

Nouns

sickness = a health problem
illness = sickness
disease = a kind of sickness, usually serious
health problem = general trouble with health

1. Malaria and tuberculosis are dangerous _____*diseases*_____ .

2. The cold is a very common _____*sickness or illness or health problem*_____

3. Although the doctor couldn't find any one _____*health problem*_____ , my
   aunt still has _____*sickness or illness*_____

Verbs

to treat = to try to make a health condition better
to cure = to make a disease go away
to heal = to become whole; to improve a health condition like a broken bone or a scratch

1. The doctor is _____*to treating*_____ her poor health with massage, good nutrition, and
   herbs, but she still doesn't feel very good.

2. A psychic _____*cures*_____ my cousin's asthma. He is completely well now.

3. My friend's broken arm is _____*healing*_____ very nicely now.

Natural childbirth class.

Using Restrictive Relative Clauses

Good writers combine short sentences with relative pronouns to make longer, more natural sentences. Combine these sentences with the relative pronouns *who* or *that*.

1. There are many women in the United States and Canada. ~~They~~ *Who* want to give birth (have babies) in their own homes. _____

   There are many women who want to give birth in their own homes in the United States and Canada.

2. Women give birth in their homes with the help of midwives. ~~They~~ *Who* live far from a hospital or don't like the hospital environment. _____

   Women (who live far from a hospital or don't like the hospital environment) give birth in their homes with the help of midwives.

3. Midwives are trained men and women. ~~They~~ *Who* have special licenses to help women

with the births of their children. _____

_____

_____

4. Midwives are often better than doctors with normal births. *Who* They have years of experience. _____

_____

5. Women often have midwives to help them with their births. *Who* They want to use natural
childbirth. _____

_____

6. Natural childbirth is a method. Women who want to give birth without drugs or
anesthesia use it. *That* _____

_____

_____

H.W. 8/9

(adj. 3.j) — no commas

Complete these sentences with relative clauses that begin with *who* or *that*.

1. There are many traditional remedies *that help more than modern*
medicines. (that cure sickness) (that treat people mentally)

2. People *who grew up in ancient time* _____ often
use herbs to treat diseases. *(live in Asia often)*

3. One remedy *that isn't for good for human beings*
isn't used very often in modern times. *(who cured many serious diseases by*

4. I knew a woman *who held a million dollars*. *playing)*

5. There are many plants *that are used for medicines to cure*
a disease.

Using Transitional Words and Phrases: in addition, for example, and however

Transitional words and phrases help unify a paragraph. They explain the connection
between two or more thoughts. They often come at the beginning of a sentence.

Adding Information: *in addition*

In addition is similar to *and* and *also*. Use *in addition* when you are adding information after a long sentence or after several sentences.

Example: People used to drink special teas to cure many illnesses. Herbalists made some of these teas from the bark of certain trees. *In addition*, they sometimes made a cream with certain kinds of bark to put on cuts and bruises.

Giving examples: *for example*

Use *for example* when you want to give specific examples.

Example: Many people go to psychic healers. *For example*, my cousin went to a psychic healer who cured his high fever with the touch of her hands.

Giving contrasting information: *however*

However is similar to *but*, but it often appears in more formal writing.

Example: Some psychic healers can cure many diseases. *However*, others just take people's money and don't help them.

Complete the sentences with *in addition*, *for example*, or *however*.

1. There are many Chinese acupuncturists in Canada. Many of them studied acupuncture in China and then immigrated to Canada. ___*In addition*___, many Canadian doctors are now giving acupuncture treatments.

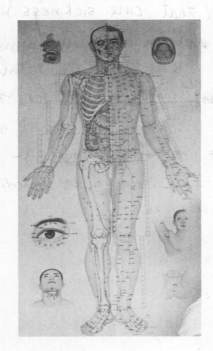

Preparing herbal medicines on San Blas islands, near Panama.

2. I often drink herbal teas when I am sick. _____*However*_____, if I am very sick
I take modern medicine.

3. Some people in California use many traditional treatments. _____*for example*_____,
they use Indian remedies and treatments that immigrants brought from their countries.

4. My grandmother often goes to an old lady who gives her strange treatments. _____*However*_____, these treatments don't usually help her.

5. I take lemon juice for colds. I put it in a cup of warm water and drink it several times a day. _____*For example*_____, I take it for sore throats and fevers.

Giving Reasons and Examples

H.W.
7/20/90

Read this paragraph and answer the questions.

drugs store

You don't have to spend a lot of money at a pharmacy to treat a cold. <u>There are many old remedies that are just as good as the newer ones.</u> For example, my grandmother always advised us to drink honey and lemon juice in hot water when we had coughs. People (who study natural medicine now) say that lemon juice is good for colds because it kills germs. I'm not sure why honey is good for colds, but I always feel better after I take it. In addition, my mother used to put me in a room full of steam to help me breathe better when I had a cold. Because scientists don't know how to kill viruses, there aren't any cures for colds, which viruses cause. I think honey, lemon juice, and steam are <u>safer than</u> chemicals with long names I can't pronounce.

1. Does the underlined sentence give a reason or an example? _____

2. What expression introduces the first example of a traditional treatment? _____
   drink honey and lemon juice.

3. What was the second example of a traditional treatment? What words showed that it was additional information? _put it in a room +_
   _____

4. *Because* introduces clauses of reason or purpose. An infinitive (*to* + *VERB*) can also show purpose. Find an example of an infinitive expression that shows purpose.
   Because it kill germ   to put   to help
   to kill viruses.

Using Correct Form

Using Commas with Transitional Words and Phrases

Transitional words often begin sentences. A comma usually comes after a transitional word.

Example: In addition, people use hot peppers to treat colds.   *mod*

After each sentence write another sentence that begins with *for example, in addition,* or *however.* Put commas after the transitional words.

1. I don't use traditional treatments. _However, I think that_
   a traditional treatments can improve health, more than
   absorb mentally modern treatments

2. Many herbal teas are good for the digestion. _____
   For example,

3. She went to a nutritionist. _____
   _____

4. Psychologists can help you with many problems. _However, their help_
   still limit

5. It's important to eat healthful foods. _On example,_
   _____

germ = A microscopic organism that causes disease

viruse = a submicroscopic disease causing agent.

Add commas to this paragraph. Remember to use commas after transitional words and after dependent clauses that begin sentences. Also use commas before conjunctions when you combine two complete sentences.

Some people can cure themselves of cancer with traditional treatments. For example, I know a woman who cured herself of cancer by fasting. She didn't eat for one month, and then she slowly began to eat again. When she completed the fast, she had completely cured herself of cancer. In addition, I read about a man who cured his cancer using an old Chinese diet. As soon as he started the diet, he began to get better.

PART III. WRITING AND EDITING

Writing the First Draft

Now write your paragraph, about traditional treatments that people in your culture use. Give reasons and examples when you can. Use these expressions:

1. examples: *for example*
2. reasons: *because, to +* verb
3. additional reasons or examples: *in addition, also*

Give your opinion in the last sentence of your paragraph.

Editing Practice

Edit this paragraph and rewrite it correctly.

Jethro Kloss was an herbalist. He treated many Americans that doctors couldn't help. He write a book that it was very important in the movement back to traditional treatments. Mr. Kloss encouraged the use of natural remedy. Mr. Kloss lived in Wisconsin. Example, he said that a good diet with

Herbal remedies.

plenty of fruit and vegetables was very important. As a treatment for disease, he recommend special cold and hot water baths. He advised his patients to get a lot of exercise. He recommended massage. Because he knew about hundreds of herbs he was one of the most famous herbalists in the United States.

Now look at the paragraph carefully. Check it for:

1. **Content**
   a. Is the information interesting?
   b. Are there reasons and examples in the paragraph?

2. **Organization**
   a. Does the topic sentence give the main idea of the paragraph?
   b. Are all the sentences about the topic of the paragraph?
   c. Does the writer include enough information?

3. **Cohesion and style**
   a. Does the writer use relative clauses correctly?
   b. Does the writer use transitional words and phrases correctly?
   c. Does the writer use synonyms correctly?

4. **Grammar**
   a. Does the writer use correct noun forms?
   b. Does the writer use correct verb tenses?

5. Correct form
   a. Are there commas after transitional words and after dependent clauses?

Discuss the corrections you made with other students.

Editing Your Writing

Now edit the paragraph you wrote. Check it for content, organization, cohesion, style, and form.

Writing the Second Draft

After you edit your paragraph, rewrite it neatly. Use good handwriting and correct form.

PART IV. COMMUNICATING THROUGH WRITING

Give your paragraph to your teacher for comments.

Sharing

The class can make a short book of traditional treatments throughout the world. Type or write your paragraphs neatly and make a book with them. Maybe someone in the class can draw some pictures for the book. You can give your book to another English class to read.

Using Feedback

Look at your teacher's comments. If you don't understand something, ask about it.
   Look at these symbols that many people use to correct writing.

sp The spelling is wrong.

vt The tense of the verb is wrong.

ro You wrote a *run-on* sentence. A run-on sentence is an incorrect sentence that should be two sentences: He ate only junk food and never exercised, in addition he stayed up late nearly every night.

You should move the circled part to where the arrow points.

≡ Capitalize the letter.

ww The word is wrong. Some words are almost synonyms, but each has special uses. I like to swim to rest.

Rewrite these sentences correctly.

1. many people in the Philippines drink herb teas. _____

_____

2. The healer gave (to my friend) a foot massage. _____

_____

3. Three years ago he have a stomach ache. _____

_____

4. His leg did not cure. _____

5. My friend didn't like to go to doctors, he went to a psychic. _____

_____

8 TELEVISION AND THE MEDIA

PART I. GETTING READY TO WRITE

Exploring Ideas

Look at the photos from these movies and match them with the movie categories below:

drama	comedy	horror	musical
science fiction	detective	adventure	

1. *The Godfather*

   Category: _____

2. *The African Queen*

   Category: _____

3. *The Pink Panther*

   Category: _____

4. *The Exorcist*

   Category: _____

5. *Swing Time*

   Category: _____

6. *Murder on the Orient Express*

   Category: _____

7. *Godzilla*

   Category: _____

Now discuss these questions.

1. What kind of movie do you like best?

2. What kind of movie do you like least?

3. What is your favorite movie? Who are the stars of that movie? Who are the main characters? What type of movie is it? When and where does it take place?

Building Vocabulary

1. Circle the adjectives that describe your favorite movie.

exciting	interesting	entertaining
funny	realistic	action-packed
fascinating	sad	well-written, well-directed
informative	imaginative	frightening
horrifying	touching	heart-warming

2. Who is your favorite character in the movie? What is he or she like? Circle the adjectives that describe him or her.

crazy	talkative	loyal
funny	well-informed	smart
angry	shy	well-educated
evil	talented	interesting
fun-loving	ambitious	hard-working
brave	kind	successful

3. List any other adjectives that describe this character:

_____ _____ _____

_____ _____ _____

Organizing Ideas

Limiting Information in a Summary

You are going to write a paragraph about your favorite movie. In ten minutes, write the plot of the movie. Write it as a list of events. Do not worry about grammar or form. If there are any words you don't know, write them in your native language.

Now look at this list of events from the movie *E.T.: The Extra-Terrestrial.*

1. Spaceship lands on earth.
2. E.T. leaves ship to collect samples of plants.

3. Men arrive to search for ship.
4. E.T. hides from men.
5. Spaceship must leave without E.T.
6. E.T. goes to Elliot's home to look for food.
7. Elliot sees E.T. in his back yard.
8. Everyone laughs at Elliot when he tells them about E.T.
9. Elliot waits for E.T. to come back.
10. E.T. comes back and Elliot hides him in his bedroom.
11. Elliot shows E.T. to his brother.
12. His brother promises not to tell anyone.
13. Elliot tells his brother that he is going to keep E.T.
14. Elliot and E.T. become good friends.
15. Scientists are watching Elliot because they think he has E.T.
16. E.T. becomes homesick.
17. E.T. makes a machine to contact his home.

18. Elliot helps E.T. send a message to his home.
19. E.T. and Elliot become very sick.
20. The scientists capture E.T. and Elliot.
21. E.T. dies.
22. E.T. comes back to life.
23. Elliot helps E.T. escape from the scientists.
24. Elliot takes E.T. to the woods on his bicycle.
25. E.T. meets the spaceship that will take him home.
26. E.T. leaves earth.

A good movie summary should tell the reader the problem and the events that lead to the solution. Now read these two summaries. Which is a better summary of the movie *E.T.?* Why?

    E.T. is from outer space. Some scientists are trying to capture him. No one believes that Elliot saw E.T. They all laugh at him. Elliot shows E.T. to his brother. His brother promises not to tell anyone. E.T. wants to go home. The scientists capture E.T. E.T. escapes and meets a spaceship. The spaceship takes him home.

    <u>E.T.: The Extra-Terrestrial</u> is the story of the friendship of a young boy and a creature from outer space. When E.T.'s spaceship leaves without him, he meets Elliot, who becomes his friend. E.T. likes Elliot, but he is very homesick, so Elliot decides to help him contact his friends. This is not easy because some scientists are searching for E.T. in order to study him. Elliot and E.T. escape from the scientists by bicycle. They go to the woods to meet the spaceship that will take E.T. home.

Look back at the list of events you wrote from your favorite movie. Which events are the most important? Are there any sentences about events that you can combine?

Including Important Information in a Summary

The paragraph that you write should have more information than a summary of the events in the movie. The paragraph that follows includes all of the information in the list below. Read the paragraph and find all the information listed.

1. the problem _____

2. where the movie takes place _____

3. the result _____

4. the main characters _____

5. when the movie takes place _____

6. type of movie _____

<u>Raiders of the Lost Ark</u>:
A Thrilling Adventure

One of my favorite movies is the action-packed adventure story, <u>Raiders of the Lost Ark</u>. It is an entertaining film that takes place in the Middle East during World War II. At the beginning of the movie, the American government learns that the Nazis are looking for an ancient relic that has extraordinary powers. The government asks Indiana Jones, an eccentric archeology professor, to find the relic before the Nazis do. This is not an easy job because Indiana's old enemy, Leclerc, is helping the Nazis. Indiana and his girl-friend Marion, the stubborn but fearless daughter of one of Indiana's old friends, must escape from death again and again. Even when their enemies throw them into a room full of snakes, they find a way out. By the end of the film

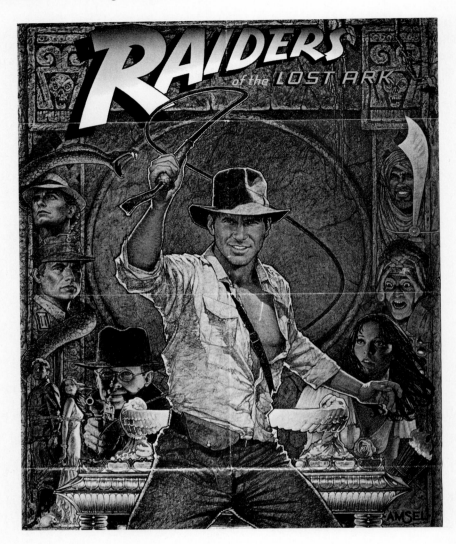

everyone is satisfied. The American government has the

relic, Indiana and Marion have each other, and the audience

had a great time.

Now look at your summary of your favorite movie. Make a list of any other information you would like to add.

Writing a Title
If you give your paragraph an interesting title, people will want to read it. Look at the following titles. Which movies would you like to read about?

1. *Star Trek III:* My Favorite Movie

2. *E.T.:* A Good Movie

3. *Friday the 13th:* An Unforgettable Experience

Now write a title for your paragraph. _____

_____

PART II. DEVELOPING WRITING SKILLS

Developing Cohesion and Style

Using Adjectives

Look back at the list of adjectives that describe movies in the section "Building Vocabulary." Find appropriate adjectives to add to these sentences.

1. *Star Wars* is a science-fiction movie. _____

_____

2. *Friday the Thirteenth* is a thriller that takes place at a summer camp. _____

_____

3. *48 Hours* is a police movie in which a policeman and a criminal work together to

find a killer. _____

_____

4. *Gandhi* is a drama about the life of the famous Indian leader. _____

_____

Now write a similar sentence about your favorite movie.

_____

_____

Look back at the list of adjectives that describe characters. Find appropriate adjectives to add to these sentences.

1. In the movie *Star Wars*, R2D2 is a robot. _____

_____

2. E.T. is a visitor from another planet. _____

_____

3. Hercule Poirot is a detective in the film *Murder on the Orient Express.* _____

_____

Sometimes you may want to use more than one adjective. You can separate two or more adjectives with a comma.

Examples: E.T. is a friendly, lovable creature from outer space.

In the movie *Rocky,* the main character is a handsome, determined boxer.

Look at these sentences. Put a comma between the two adjectives.

1. *Gandhi* is the story of a wise kind man who leads India to freedom.

2. In *Flashdance,* Jennifer Beals plays a beautiful talented dancer.

3. *Poltergeist* tells the story of a family that has problems with evil destructive ghosts.

4. *Stripes* is about two crazy fun-loving boys who decide to join the army.

However, when there are two contrasting adjectives, you can separate them with *but.*

Example: In *Star Wars,* Han Solo is a brave *but* self-centered pilot.

Put the word *but* in the appropriate places in the sentences.

1. In *The Pink Panther,* Inspector Clouseau is a stupid successful police detective.

2. *Frankenstein* is the story of a destructive tragic monster.

3. The Godfather is an evil loyal man.

4. In *E.T.,* the boy Elliot is sensitive brave.

Now write sentences that describe the main characters in your favorite movie. Use more than one adjective in each sentence.

Using Appositives

An appositive modifies a noun and follows it directly.

Example: Han Solo, *a brave but self-centered pilot,* is one of the heroes of *Star Wars.*

Can you find any appositives in the paragraph about *Raiders of the Lost Ark?* Underline them.

Combine the following sentences; use appositives.

1. The movie *48 Hours* is my favorite. It is the story of the friendship between a policeman and a criminal. _____

_____

2. Gandhi changed the history of India. He was a great leader. _____

3. Brooke Shields starred in *The Blue Lagoon.* She is a beautiful young American actress. _____

4. Han Solo needed help from R2D2. R2D2 was a robot. _____

5. Steven Spielberg directed *Close Encounters of the Third Kind.* It is the story of an alien's visit to earth. _____

Using the Historical Present Tense

Look back at the paragraph about *Raiders of the Lost Ark.* What tense is it in? You can use the present tense to talk about events in the past. This is the "historical present." Look at the paragraph below and complete it with the correct forms of the verbs in parentheses. Use the historical present.

Blue Thunder _____ (be) a police adventure film. In the movie, Roy Scheider _____ (play) Frank Murphey, a helicopter pilot who _____ (work) for the Los Angeles police department. The police department _____ (purchase) Blue Thunder, an extremely advanced helicopter, to help them guard the 1984 Olympics. The police _____ (believe) that this helicopter is the "ultimate weapon." Its guns can _____ (shoot) 4,000 bullets a minute and it can _____ (show) the pilot objects on the ground which _____ (be) too small for him to see. When Murphey _____ (take) Blue Thunder on a test flight, he _____ (discover) a government plan to use the aircraft against ordinary people. He then _____ (try) to stop them.

Using Correct Form

Punctuating Titles

Titles of movies are underlined (or in italics in printed material). All the important words in a title (of a movie, book, etc.) begin with a capital letter. Small words such as *in, a, the, to, at* do not begin with a capital letter unless they are the first words in the title.

Examples: The Adventures of Tarzan
                 Raiders of the Lost Ark

Punctuate the titles in parentheses and capitalize words that need capital letters.

1. If you like frightening movies, you should see (the omen).

2. Sir Richard Attenborough directed (Gandhi).

3. (The empire strikes back) was a sequel to (star wars).

4. The most famous American movie is (gone with the wind), the story of Southern families during the Civil War.

5. I saw (indiana jones and the temple of doom) yesterday.

PART III. WRITING AND EDITING

Writing the First Draft

Now write your paragraph about your favorite movie.

Editing Practice

Edit this paragraph and rewrite it correctly.

```
              Star trek II: the Wrath Of Khan

   Star trek II is a sequel to Star Trek: The Motion picture.

But it's much better. In this science fiction adventure

film. Khan, an evil clever leader steal information about

Genesis a secret government experiment. Khan and his people

lived in exile for along time. The crew of the Enterprise

must catch Khan before he can to use it. Captain Kirk and

his crew succeeds as usually but in the end the captain lose

a good friend. Which one of the crew die? Go see the movie

and find out. I liked this movie a lot, maybe you will too.
```

Now look at the paragraph carefully. Check it for:

1. Content
   a. Is the title interesting?
   b. Does the information make you want to see the movie?

2. Organization
   a. Are there any unnecessary details?
   b. Does the paragraph have an effective topic sentence?
   c. Does the paragraph have a good concluding sentence?
   d. Does the writer present the information clearly?

3. Cohesion and style
   a. Are the verb tenses correct?
   b. Are the appositives correct?

4. Grammar
   a. Are there any sentence fragments?

5. Correct form
   a. Does the title have correct punctuation and capitalization?
   b. Did the writer use commas correctly?

Discuss the corrections you made with other students.

Editing Your Writing

Now edit the paragraph you wrote. Check it for content, organization, cohesion, style, and form.

Writing the Second Draft

After you edit your paragraph, rewrite it neatly. Use good handwriting and correct form.

PART IV. COMMUNICATING THROUGH WRITING

Give your paragraph to your teacher for comments.

Sharing

Read three of your classmates' movie reviews. Discuss which movies you would like to see and why.

Using Feedback

Look at your teacher's comments. If you don't understand something, ask about it. Then look at the paragraphs you wrote for the last three or four chapters. In what areas do you see improvement in your work? What areas still need more improvement?

9
FRIENDS AND SOCIAL LIFE

PART I. GETTING READY TO WRITE

Look at these pictures of Tony, a foreign student studying English. Then describe Tony. What has he been doing during the past year? How has he been feeling? Use the information in the pictures and add other information. Write as many sentences as you can in ten minutes.

Discuss the kind of information you wrote in your sentences. Did you write about any of the following topics? What did you say about each topic? Think of other things you can write about a student in your class. Your teacher will list them on the board.

- Family life
- Social life
- Work
- Accomplishments
- Unusual events

Write questions about the topics above. Then interview a student about his or her life in the past year. Take notes on the information your partner gives you.

Building Vocabulary

Add other words and expressions you used in your discussions and interview to the list on page 104.

Nouns	Verbs	Adjectives	Other
accomplishment	accomplish	exhausted	_____
hobby	attend	fascinating	_____
recreation	_____	_____	_____
_____	_____	_____	_____
_____	_____	_____	_____
_____	_____	_____	_____
_____	_____	_____	_____
_____	_____	_____	_____

Organizing Ideas

You are going to write a paragraph about a student in your class for a class newsletter. The paragraph will tell what the student has been doing for the past year.

Writing Topic Sentences

Topic sentences are often in the present perfect tense because it is common to use the present perfect to introduce a subject. Which of these sentences are good general topic sentences for a paragraph about Tony's life during the past year? Circle the numbers of those sentences. Which sentence do you think is the most interesting? Put a check by it.

1. Tony Prado has had a busy life this year.

2. Tony Prado has been married since June.

3. This year Tony Prado has had so much to do that he has felt like a juggler.

4. Tony Prado has learned a lot of English this year.

5. During the past year Tony Prado has gotten married, worked at two jobs, played soccer, and studied English.

6. During the past year Tony Prado has had a full but happy life.

Now write a topic sentence for your paragraph. Use the present perfect or present perfect continuous tense._____

_____

Organizing Information in a Paragraph

There are several ways to organize your paragraph. Two ways are:

1. You can begin with more important activities such as work, and you can end with less important activities such as hobbies or interesting events.
2. You can begin with difficult activities and end with more enjoyable activities.

Look at the notes about Tony's life. Work in small groups and arrange them in order. Use one of the two types of organization above.

```
goes to English classes--has no time to study

works in uncle's factory--makes him tired

got married in June

rides bikes with his wife

works evenings in a beauty salon

plays soccer with friends
```

Now look at your notes from your interview and arrange them in the order you think you are going to write about. Discuss the order with your partner.

Writing a Concluding Sentence

The final sentence of a paragraph sometimes summarizes the paragraph or leads into the future. Look at these examples of possible final sentences.

1. In November Tony's wife is going to have a baby, and then he will have another thing to juggle in his busy schedule.
2. With her new English skills, Sonia is hoping to get a better job.
3. Parvin says that it's a full-time job to take care of her kids, but she can't wait till they are in school and she can get a job that pays money.
4. Satoshi is going to return to Japan and use his English in his engineering work.

Now write a final sentence you could use in your paragraph._____

_____

PART II. DEVELOPING WRITING SKILLS

Developing Cohesion and Style

Selecting the Correct Tense
It's important for each sentence to be in the correct tense. You can use this chart to check your verb tenses.

Contrast of Verb Tenses

Simple present	A repeated or habitual action in the present. *Example:* Mina studies English in Austin, Texas.
Present continuous	An action or situation that is *in progress* in the present. *Example:* Mina is studying and working at the same time this quarter.
Past	A completed action or state. *Example:* Mina came to Austin three months ago.
Present perfect	An action or, more usually, a state (with verbs like *be, have, feel, know*) that began in the past and continues in the present. Often appears with *for* and *since* + time expression. *Example:* Mina has known her friend Salima since 1982; she has known her friend Sally for one month.
Present perfect continuous	An action that began in the past and continues in the present; often appears with *for* and *since* + time expression. *Example:* Mina has been working part time in the school cafeteria since she arrived (for three months).

Complete this paragraph with the correct tenses of the verbs in parentheses. Remember that we often use the present perfect or present perfect continuous to introduce a subject and then use the present tense to talk about it further.

This year Tony _____ (have) so much to do he

_____ (feel) like a juggler. He _____ (get

married) in June and he and wife are very happy together. He _____

(work) in his uncle's factory since April. It _____ (be) hard work,

because he _____ (have to load) trucks and he

_____(get) very tired. In addition, he _____

(work) a few evenings a week as a hairdresser because he _____
(need) to save money. He also _____ (take) English classes at a
community college near his home. He _____ (enjoy) the class, but
he _____ (be) so busy he _____ (not have)
much time to study. Tony's life _____ (not be) all work, however.
In fact, he still _____ (find) time to enjoy a few sports. He
_____ (play) soccer with some friends every Sunday. In addition,
he and his wife often _____ (ride) bikes together. But she is
pregnant now and _____ (have) a baby in four months. Then
Tony _____ (have) another thing to juggle in his busy schedule.

Using Transitional Words and Phrases
However, in addition, also

The expressions *however, in addition,* and *also* help unify the sentences in a paragraph.
Find these expressions in the paragraph about Tony and underline them. Then answer
the questions.

1. Which two expressions do you use when you give additional information? _____

_____

2. Which expression do you use when you give contrasting information? _____

In the paragraph about Tony, is this expression at the beginning or end of the sen-

tence? _____ Can it be in another position? _____

In fact

We use *in fact* when we give facts that show that the sentence before is true.

Example: Tony has been very busy. *In fact,* he's been working at two jobs.

Add *in fact* or *however* to these sentences.

1. Tony has been working very hard. He works from 8:00 in the morning until 9:00 at

night. _____

_____

2. Tony has been working very hard. He still finds time to play soccer every week.

_____

_____

3. Ralph has been doing well, and he likes his English class a lot. He's been studying so much that he isn't sleeping well. _____

_____

_____

4. Ralph has been doing well in his English class. He went from Level 2 to Level 4 last month. _____

_____

Use the information in the pictures to make sentences with *in fact* or *however.*

1. Angela has been relaxing this summer. _____

_____ every day.

2. Angela has been relaxing this summer. _____

_____ twice a week too.

3. Khalil has been taking care of his children this summer.

_____ every afternoon.

4. Khalil has been taking care of his children this summer.

_____ every Saturday.

Look at your notes and write some pairs of sentences for your paragraph. Begin the second sentence of each pair with *in addition, also, however,* or *in fact.*

_____

_____

_____

_____

_____

_____

Stating Results with so . . . that

You can combine sentences giving reasons and results.

    Reason   *Result*

Tony has been busy.   +   He has felt like a juggler.   =

Tony has been *so* busy *that* he has felt like a juggler.

Combine these sentences using *so . . . that.*

1. Jane has been busy. She hasn't had much time to study. _____

_____

2. Reiko was happy. She cried. _____

3. Chi Wang has been working hard. He falls asleep in class. _____

_____

4. Nick has been having much fun. He is seldom homesick. _____

_____

5. Sonia's daughter has been sick. She had to take her to the hospital _____.

_____

_____

Can you write any sentences with *so . . . that* for your paragraph? Write them here.

_____

_____

_____

_____

Using Correct Form

Using Commas with Transitional Words and Phrases

Commas separate *in addition, however,* and *in fact* from the rest of a sentence.

Examples: In fact, she won a skiing award.
  She has not been practicing recently, however.

Do not use commas with *also* when it is in the middle of a sentence.

Example: She's also been skating a lot.

Add commas to these sentences if necessary.

1. Pierre has not been to New York yet however.
2. In fact he has been going to parties every weekend.
3. He has also been studying karate.
4. However he has met someone nice.

5. In fact they have been going out since August.

6. However she has been getting to know some of the other students in her class.

Using Long Forms in Formal Writing

When English speakers write formally, they don't use as many contractions as when they speak—instead, they use long forms. Here are some examples of contractions and their long forms:

he has → he's	he has not → he hasn't
they have → they've	they have not → they haven't
it is → it's	it is not → it's not, it isn't

Write these sentences without contractions.

1. He's been playing in a band. _____

2. They haven't moved yet. _____

3. They're not having problems with Canadian customs. _____

_____

4. Recently she's been planning a party. _____

5. It's difficult work. _____

6. She's been getting dates from a computer dating service. _____

_____

Spelling Present and Past Participles Correctly

Write the *-ing* form and the past participle of these words. For rules for adding *-ing*, see Appendix 1 at the back of this book.

	-*ing* Form	Past Participle
1. work	*working*	*worked*
2. begin	_____	_____

3. study   _____   _____

4. make   _____   _____

5. find   _____   _____

6. swim   _____   _____

7. go   _____   _____

8. travel   _____   _____

9. come   _____   _____

10. have   _____   _____

Using Correct Capitalization

In your paragraph, remember to capitalize time words correctly. (See Appendix 2 for detailed rules.)

Capitalize months and days of the week.

Monday   Wednesday   July   September

Don't capitalize seasons.

summer   fall   winter   spring

Capitalize names of schools and businesses.

Lincoln Community College   Lucia's Bakery

University of Montreal   Internet, Inc.

Don't capitalize kinds of schools, businesses, or jobs.

a bakery   a baker

an export company   an accountant

a community college   a musician

Don't capitalize school subjects except languages.

business math   French

biology   English

Write these sentences with correct capitalization.

1. Pablo has been studying computer science and english at northwestern college since january. _____

_____

2. Anna works as a dietician at randolph college. _____

_____

3. In september Van got a job as a mail clerk at a bank. _____

_____

4. Tessa has been studying fashion design every tuesday and thursday evening.

_____

5. Irena has been working with the jones plumbing company since the fall.

_____

PART III. WRITING AND EDITING

Writing the First Draft

Now write your paragraph about a classmate. Use your topic sentence and notes. Also use transitional expressions to unify your paragraph.

Editing Practice

Edit this paragraph and rewrite it correctly.

Marta Rodriguez has have a very interesting year. Last June she graduate from a tourism development course in Mexico. She received a scholarship to study english, and has ben attending classes here at the university of Ottawa since September. Marta is twenty-five years old. She's, also, been traveling in Canada and the United States. She love dance and spends at least two nights a week at the disco. She visits hotels to study the different management systems, and has learnned a lot. Fact, she says that one day in a hotel is better than ten days in a classroom. However Marta hasn't spend all her time in Canada at work. She also find time, to develop a close friendship with the manager of a big hotel here in Ottawa. She is hoping to get to know him better.

Now look at the paragraph carefully. Check it for:

1. Content
   a. Is the information interesting?
   b. Is all the information in the paragraph important?

2. Organization
   a. Does the topic sentence give the main idea of the paragraph?
   b. Are the sentences well organized?
   c. Does the paragraph have a good concluding sentence?

3. Cohesion and style
   a. Are the verb tenses correct?
   b. Did the writer use transitional expressions correctly?
   c. Did the writer use *so . . . that* correctly?

4. Grammar
   a. Did the writer use correct verb forms?

5. Correct form
   a. Did the writer use commas correctly?
   b. Did the writer spell the verb forms correctly?
   c. Did the writer use correct capitalization?

Discuss the corrections you made with other students.

Editing Your Writing

Now edit the paragraph you wrote. Check it for content, organization, cohesion, style, and form.

Writing the Second Draft

After you edit your paragraph, rewrite it neatly. Use good handwriting and correct form.

PART IV. COMMUNICATING THROUGH WRITING

Give your paragraph to your teacher for comments.

Sharing

As a class, collect all the paragraphs you wrote to make a class newsletter.

Using Feedback

Look at your teacher's comments. If you don't understand something, ask about it. Then discuss these questions.

1. What have you learned in your writing class?

2. How do you feel about writing now? Do you enjoy it? Do you think it's difficult?

3. Which step of the writing process do you like? Which step don't you like?

4. What do you think you need to practice more?

5. Have you found anything that makes writing easier for you? Tell the rest of the class about it.

6. Is there anything you would like to change in the writing class? What is it?

7. Are you doing enough writing? Would you like to do more or less?

10
CUSTOMS, CELEBRATIONS, AND HOLIDAYS

PART I. GETTING READY TO WRITE

Exploring Ideas

Look at the photographs and discuss them. What do you know about the holidays the people in the photos are celebrating?

What are the most important holidays in your country or culture? When do people celebrate these holidays? How do they celebrate them? Complete the following chart.

Holiday	Time of Year	Activities	Description of Activities

Upper left: Christmas, Sweden.
Upper right: New Year's, China.
Lower left: Carnaval, Brazil.
Lower right: Saudi Arabian National Day.

117

_____

_____

_____

_____

Look at your list of holidays. How could you divide them into groups? Try dividing them into seasons first (winter holidays, summer holidays, etc.).

_____

_____

_____

_____

_____

_____

_____

_____

Now think of other ways to group them.

Building Vocabulary

Add other words you used to describe holidays to this list.

Nouns	Verbs	Adjectives	Other
celebration	celebrate	traditional	_____
commemoration	commemorate	joyous	_____
parade	_____	_____	_____
fireworks	_____	_____	_____
tradition	_____	_____	_____
_____	_____	_____	_____
_____	_____	_____	_____
_____	_____	_____	_____

Organizing Ideas

You are going to write a paragraph about holidays in your culture.

Categorizing and Making an Outline

Here is an example of the notes that one student made about holidays in her country.

Christmas	Washington's Birthday	Halloween
New Year's	Valentine's Day	Easter
Thanksgiving	Memorial Day	Passover
July 4	Labor Day	Rosh Hashana

She decided to divide the holidays into three categories:

1. political holidays
2. religious holidays
3. traditional holidays

Some people feel that it is easier to organize their ideas in outline form. Before she began to write her paragraph, she made an outline like this:

I. Holidays in the United States

   A. Political holidays

      1. Independence Day

      2. Presidents' Day

      3. Memorial Day

      4. Labor Day

   B. Traditional holidays

      1. Thanksgiving

      2. New Year's

      3. Halloween

      4. Valentine's Day

   C. Religious holidays

      1. Christian holidays

         a. Christmas

         b. Easter

2. Jewish holidays

  a. Passover

  b. Rosh Hashana

Does your country have any political holidays? Traditional holidays? Religious holidays? Make an outline like the one above.

The student decided to write about political holidays, so she added more information to her outline. Here is her outline; some of the items are missing.

I. Holidays in the United States

  A. Political holidays

   1. Independence Day

      a. Fourth of July

      b. _____

      c. Fireworks

      d. Picnics, barbecues

   2. _____

      a. Last weekend in May

      b. Commemorate the American soldiers who died in all wars

      c. _____

      d. Parades

      e. Put flags and flowers on graves

   3. Labor Day

      a. _____

      b. Honor American workers

      c. _____

    d. Parades

    e. Picnics

4. _____

    a. George Washington

    b. _____

    c. Martin Luther King, Jr.

Fourth of July parade.

Read this paragraph, then fill in the outline with the information that is missing.

Holidays in the United States

    There are three types of holidays in the United States: political holidays, traditional holidays, and religious holidays. There are more political holidays than any other type. The most important political holiday is Independence Day, the Fourth of July. On this day we celebrate our independence from Great Britain. Most people spend the day with their family and friends. Picnics and barbecues are very popular. In addition, almost every city and town has a fireworks display at night. Another very important political holiday is Memorial Day. On this holiday we commemorate all the soldiers who died for our country. Many towns and cities have parades, and some people go to cemeteries and put flowers or flags on the soldiers' graves. Because this holiday falls on the last weekend in May, some people think of it as the beginning of the summer season. A third important political holiday is Labor Day, which we celebrate on the first Monday in September. This is the day when we honor the workers of the United States. People watch parades, go on picics, or go to the beach. For students, Labor Day is a bittersweet holiday, because when it is over they must begin school again. Besides these political holidays, we also celebrate the birthdays of George Washington, Abraham Lincoln, and Martin Luther King, Jr.

Ordering Information According to Importance

When you make a list, you often put the items in order of importance. Look back at the paragraph above. What is the most important political holiday? _____

_____

A student is going to write a paragraph about products his country exports. In what order should he mention them?

coconuts $2 million per year

cars $15 million per year

coffee $12 million per year

cloth $8 million per year

1. _____

2. _____

3. _____

4. _____

5. What kind of order is this? _____

Now look at your list of holidays and put them in order of importance.

Here is information about traditional holidays in the United States. Put the information in the correct order in the second part of the outline.

children dress in costumes
families eat turkey and other traditional foods
Halloween
February 14
January 1
Thanksgiving
people celebrate the New Year
traditional holidays
children collect candy
Valentine's Day
third Thursday in November
New Year's Day
people go to costume parties
boys and girls exchange valentines
October 31
people feel thankful for the good things in their lives

B. *traditional holidays* _____

   1. _____

      a. _____

      b. _____

   2. _____

a. _____

b. _____

3. _____

   a. _____

   b. _____

   c. _____

   d. _____

4. _____

   a. _____

   b. _____

   c. _____

Now make an outline for the type of holiday you are going to write about.

PART II. DEVELOPING WRITING SKILLS

Developing Cohesion and Style

Listing Information with in addition to, besides, another, *and* the first, second, third, last

You can use these transitional words to add information: *in addition to, besides, another,* and *the first, second, third, last.* How many of them can you find in the paragraph about holidays in the United States?

The following paragraph contains no transitional words. Complete it with the appropriate transitions. More than one answer may be correct.

Jewish people celebrate several religious holidays each year. The most important

holiday is Passover. During Passover they eat a traditional meal called a *seder.*

_____ important holiday is Yom Kippur. On this day they ask

forgiveness for their sins. _____ Yom Kippur and Passover they also

celebrate Rosh Hashana, the Jewish New Year. _____ important

Passover meal.

Jewish holiday is Hanukah, which Jewish people celebrate near the Christian holiday
of Christmas. _____ these holidays, there are several minor holidays
such as Purim.

Unifying a Paragraph with Pronouns and Pronominal Expressions

You can use pronouns to refer to things you have already mentioned so that you don't
have to repeat the same words again and again. Here is a list of the pronouns and
pronominal expressions in the paragraph about holidays in the United States. Tell what
each one refers to.

1. on this day (line 5) _____

2. on this holiday (line 10) _____

3. this holiday (line 13) _____

4. it (line 14) _____

5. this is the day (line 17) _____

6. it (line 20) _____

7. they (line 20) _____

The paragraph that follows needs more pronouns. Edit it and substitute pronouns or
pronominal expressions for *some* of the nouns. Remember that too many pronouns are
as bad as too few.

Children looking for Easter eggs.

Christians celebrate several religious holidays. In December, Christians celebrate Christmas. Christmas commemorates the birthday of Jesus Christ. On Christmas, Christians usually decorate trees and give each other presents. In addition, Christians often spend this day with their families. Easter is another important Christian holiday. Christians often give their children candy and colored eggs on Easter. Lent is not a holiday, but for Christians Lent is a special time. Lent lasts for forty days. During Lent, Christians ask for forgiveness for their sins.

Using Quantifiers

For a paragraph like the one you are going to write, you will probably need to use quantifiers, words that tell the amount of something. Some quantifiers are:

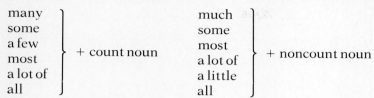

many
some
a few
most
a lot of
all
} + count noun

much
some
most
a lot of
a little
all
} + noncount noun

How many quantifiers can you find in the paragraph about holidays in the United States? Underline them.

Using Nonrestrictive Relative Clauses

In Chapter 7 you learned about restrictive relative clauses with *who* and *that*.

Examples: Ramadan is the Moslem holiday *that lasts a month.*
Moslems *who celebrate Ramadan* fast (do not eat) from sunrise to sunset during this month.

A restrictive relative clause tells you which person or thing the writer is referring to. A nonrestrictive relative clause gives additional information. This information is not necessary. You can omit a nonrestrictive relative clause, but you cannot omit a restrictive relative clause.

Example: Thanksgiving, *which falls in November,* is a time for families to get together. (nonrestrictive) Notice that you can omit the clause *which falls in November: Thanksgiving is a time for families to get together.*

Example: Christmas is the holiday *that I like best.* (restrictive)
Notice that if you omit the clause *that I like best,* the sentence seems incomplete: *Christmas is the holiday.*

In nonrestrictive relative clauses, use *which* instead of *that.*

Combine these sentences with *which* and a nonrestrictive relative clause. Insert a clause at the ∧ mark.

1. Easter ∧ is a happy holiday. Easter comes in the springtime. _____

_____

2. The Fourth of July ∧ is a time for big parades and fireworks. The Fourth of July is

Independence Day. _____

_____

_____

3. Martin Luther King Day ∧ comes in January. Martin Luther King Day is our newest holiday. _____

_____

4. Halloween ∧ is a favorite children's holiday. Halloween is an ancient British tradition.

_____

_____

5. On New Year's Day ∧ there is a famous parade in Pasadena, California. New Year's Day is the first holiday of the year. _____

_____

_____

Using Correct Form

Punctuating Nonrestrictive Relative Clauses

Use commas to separate a nonrestrictive relative clause from the rest of the sentence. If the clause comes in the middle of the sentence, use two commas.

Example: Valentine's Day, which falls on February 14, is a holiday for lovers.

If the clause comes at the end of the sentence, use only one comma.

Example: Memorial Day is in May, which is almost the beginning of the summer in the United States.

Rewrite these sentences and use commas where necessary.

1. Songkran which is the Thai New Year is on April 13.

2. Eid-e-ghorbon is a religious holiday in Iran which is a Muslim country.

3. Christmas which is an important holiday in Christian countries is usually a happy time.

4. Bastille Day which is on July 14 is a very important holiday in France.

PART III. WRITING AND EDITING

Writing the First Draft

Now write your paragraph about holidays in your culture.

Editing Practice

Edit this paragraph and rewrite it correctly.

Bastille Day, France.

traditional holidays in United States

There are four important traditional holidays in the United States. Another important traditional holiday is New Year's Eve. On New Year's eve most people go to parties. At twelve o'clock everyone shout Happy New Year! and wish their friends good luck. New Year's parties usually until late. Some not go home until the morning. The most important of these holiday Thanksgiving. Which we celebrate on the third thursday in November. this is a family holiday. Most of people spend the day with their relatives. The most important tradition on this day Thanksgiving dinner. At a traditional Thanksgiving dinner the most people eat turkey with

Children in Haloween costumes.

stuffing, cranberry sauce, and pumpkin pie. The third traditional holiday is for children. It is Halloween. On this
Halloween children dress as witches and ghosts. Most of they
go from house to house and say ''Trick or Treat.'' If the
people at the house do not give them candy, the children
will play a trick on them. But this hardly ever happens.
Almost give them candy or fruit. The next holiday is Valentine's Day which is in February.

Now look at the paragraph carefully. Check it for:

1. Content
   a. Is the information interesting?
   b. Is there enough information?

2. Organization
   a. Did you list the holidays from most important to least important?
   b. Did you give the same type of information about each holiday?

3. Cohesion and style
   a. Are the verb forms correct?
   b. Did you use the quantifiers correctly?
   c. Did you use the transitional words correctly?
   d. Did you use relative clauses correctly?

4. Grammar
   a. Are there any sentence fragments?

5. Correct form
   a. Did you punctuate the title correctly?
   b. Do the relative clauses have commas where necessary?

Discuss the corrections you made with other students.

Editing Your Writing

Now edit the paragraph you wrote. Check it for content, organization, cohesion, style, and form.

Writing the Second Draft

After you edit your paragraph, rewrite it neatly. Use good handwriting and correct form.

PART IV. COMMUNICATING THROUGH WRITING

Give your paragraph to your teacher for comments.

Sharing

Bring in pictures to illustrate different holidays your class celebrates. Put them on a bulletin board.

Using Feedback

Look at your teacher's comments. If you don't understand something, ask about it. Then, compare your first draft and your second draft. What mistakes were easy for you to find? What mistakes did you miss? Make a list of the kinds of mistakes you need to avoid.

CHAPTER

11 RECREATION

PART I. GETTING READY TO WRITE

Exploring Ideas

Look at the picture of the park and write as much as you can about it in five minutes. Tell what the people are doing and what has happened. Then discuss the picture. Answer these questions:

1. What are the people in the pictures doing?

2. Which of the activities do you like to participate in?

3. Which of the activities do you like to watch?

4. What other things do you like to do in your free time?

Now complete the following list about things you like to do.

*Outdoor
Activities*

_____
_____
_____
_____

*Indoor
Activities*

_____
_____
_____
_____

*Activities
You Like to Do
Alone*

_____
_____
_____
_____

*Activities
You Like to
Do with Others*

_____
_____
_____
_____

*Activities
You Like to
Participate in*

_____
_____
_____
_____

*Activities
You Like to
Watch*

_____
_____
_____
_____

Compare your list with those of some other students. Which activities are you most interested in? Which activities are they most interested in? Which activity would you like to recommend to other students?

Building Vocabulary

Add other words you used in your discussion to this list.

Nouns	Verbs	Adjectives	Other
roller skating	roller skate	thrilling	_____
soccer	play soccer	relaxing	_____
listening to music	listen to music	fun	_____
spectator	participate in	exciting	_____
jazz band	benefit	enjoyable	_____
benefit	stroll	peaceful	_____
fun		entertaining	_____
_____	_____	pleasant	_____
_____	_____	inexpensive	_____
_____	_____	spectacular	_____
_____	_____	sensational	_____
_____	_____	easy	_____
_____	_____	_____	_____
_____	_____	_____	_____
_____	_____	_____	_____

What does each of the words in the column *Adjectives* mean? Can you add other adjectives to the list?

Organizing Ideas

Organizing Information by Answering what?, who?, where?, when?, how?, and why?

You are going to write a paragraph about an activity you like and want to recommend to your classmates. One way to organize a paragraph is to ask *what?, who?, where?, when?, how?,* and *why?* about your idea. Look at the notes that a student made about roller skating.

Roller Skating

1. What activity do you want to recommend? *roller skating*

2. Who can participate in this activity? *People of any age. Many families like to roller skate together. Young people often skate.*

3. Where and when can they do it? *Outdoors in parks during the day, indoor rinks in the evening*

4. How can they do it? *Can rent skates in parks or indoor rinks. If they do it often, they can buy skates.*

5. Why would they like to do it? *It's an easy sport to learn. You can do it alone or with other people. It's fun to do to music. Not expensive. Good exercise.*

Now answer the questions about the activity you are going to write about.

1. What activity do you want to recommend? _____

2. Who can participate in this activity? _____

_____

3. Where and when can they do it? _____

_____

_____

4. How can they do it? _____

_____

_____

5. Why would they like to do it? _____

_____

_____

Writing Topic Sentences

In a paragraph where you make a recommendation, you want the topic sentence to get the reader interested in what you're going to say. Look at these topic sentences for a paragraph recommending roller skating. Notice that sometimes the writer needed two sentences to get the reader interested. Which topic sentences do you like? Why do you like them?

1. Roller skating used to be just for kids, but now thousands of adults are finding that it is a great sport.

2. Would you like to try a sport that is easy to learn, a lot of fun, and not expensive? Then roller skating may be for you.

3. Roller skating is a nice sport.

4. One of the most exciting feelings in the world is gliding through the park on a sunny day on roller skates.

5. I like to roller skate because it is fun.

6. If you want to try a sport that's great for the whole family, then you may want to try roller skating.

There are certain structures that commonly appear in topic sentences that try to interest the reader in the paragraph.

1. One of the most _____ I've ever _____ is _____ .

2. One of the most _____ in the world is _____ .

3. If you want _____ , then _____ .

4. Would you like _____ ? Then _____ .

Read this paragraph and then write four different topic sentences using the structures on page 136.

The Benefits of Walking

_____ . Walking may not seem fascinating, but it can be. When you walk, you move slowly, so you can see the world around you. Walking is great because you can do it anytime and anywhere. An evening walk through the streets of a big city can be just as enjoyable as a morning stroll on a country road. In addition, you don't need any fancy equipment to participate in this activity. If you have a good pair of shoes, you're ready to go. Another benefit of this pastime is that you can enjoy it with friends or alone. You also don't have to worry about winning or losing. Just getting there is enough.

Topic sentences:

1. _____
   _____

2. _____
   _____

3. _____
   _____

4. _____
   _____

   Now write a topic sentence or sentences that will make a reader interested in the activity you are going to write about. You can use the structures above or think of another way to get the interest of the reader.

_____

_____

PART II. DEVELOPING WRITING SKILLS

Developing Cohesion and Style

Unifying a Paragraph with Synonyms and Pronouns

One way of unifying a paragraph is to refer to the same word or topic several times. Sometimes you use the same word for the topic, and sometimes you use synonyms or other words to refer to it. Find these words in the paragraph about walking and underline them.

it	this pastime	a morning stroll
this activity	an evening walk	

Insert these words into the paragraph that follows.

roller skating	this activity
this sport	it

Follow these directions:

1. Don't repeat *roller skating* in the same sentence. Use *it* or *this sport/activity* the second time.

2. If you haven't used the word *roller skating* in a few sentences, repeat it.

Dancing to Music

One of the most exciting feelings in the world is gliding through the park on a sunny day on roller skates. People of any age can participate in _____. Many families like to roller skate together, and _____ is the perfect activity for students who want to feel free after a long day in the classroom. Another benefit of _____ is that you can do _____ in an indoor rink or on the sidewalks of a park. If you want to try _____ before buying skates, you can rent them in rinks or stands near parks. _____ is an easy sport to learn. You can do it alone or with friends. _____ is also not expensive and _____ is good exercise. But the thing I like best about _____ is that you can skate to music. _____ is like dancing on wheels.

Using Gerunds

When writing about recreational activities, you can use gerunds as subjects, objects, and objects of prepositions.

> *Examples:* *Roller skating* is easy to learn. (subject)
> I enjoy *walking.* (object)
> You can try it before *buying* skates. (object of preposition)

Find the gerunds in the paragraph above and in the one about walking. Are they subjects? Objects? Objects of prepositions? Does a singular or plural verb follow the subjects?

Complete these sentences with gerund phrases.

1. _____ is one of the most exciting sports I've ever watched.

2. After _____ it feels great to take a hot shower.

3. I don't enjoy _____ .

4. Every weekend I look forward to _____ .

5. One of the benefits of _____ is that it's good exercise.

6. I've often dreamed of _____ .

7. Have you ever tried _____ ?

8. Last month he started _____ .

Using the Pronoun you

In informal writing English speakers often use the pronoun *you* when talking about people in general.

Examples: *You* can do this activity indoors or outdoors.
I'm sure *you* will find that parachuting is exciting.

Circle all the uses of the pronoun *you* in the paragraphs about walking and roller skating. Then write a few sentences for your paragraph using *you* to refer to people in general.

Using Adjectives + Infinitive Complements

When talking about recreational activities, you can use an adjective + *to* + a verb.

Examples: It's *necessary to use* the correct equipment for American football.
Volleyball is *easy to learn.*

Make at least six sentences with these adjectives and appropriate activities.

Example: It's easy to learn to play volleyball.

1. easy	a. play soccer
2. fun	b. watch baseball
3. exciting	c. learn to play table tennis
4. relaxing	d. listen to rock music
5. difficult	e. ride bicycles
6. enjoyable	f. learn to roller skate

_____

_____

_____

_____

_____

_____

_____

_____

Using Correct Form

Forming the Superlative of Adjectives

Remember to add *-est* to most one-syllable adjectives and to adjectives ending in *-y*. Use *most* to form the superlative of other adjectives. For rules on the spelling of adjectives with *-est*, see Appendix 1 at the back of this book.

Examples: big → biggest   easy → easiest
            spectacular → most spectacular

Write the superlative of these words with *the*.

Example: popular   <u>the most popular</u>

1. nice   _____
2. exciting _____
3. good   _____
4. fascinating _____
5. relaxing _____
6. enjoyable _____
7. thrilling _____
8. cheap   _____

PART III. WRITING AND EDITING

Writing the First Draft

Now write your paragraph about a favorite activity. Use the notes and topic sentence you have written. Look at the titles of the paragraphs on walking and roller skating. Write an interesting title for your paragraph.

Editing Practice

Edit this paragraph and rewrite it correctly.

Mind Travel

If you would like learn the inexpensivest, the most fun, and most fascinating activity in the world, try daydreaming, the lazy person's sport. They can visit distant lands, win games, and meet interesting people, all in the comfort of your own home. You no need any special equipment daydreaming. With just a good imagination, you are ready begin. Is easy learning. It is best to do it alone with closed eyes, but I have had many successful daydreams in crowded classrooms with my eyes wide open. I don't like my science classes at all. Daydream is also fun while you are walking, riding the bus, or listening to boring friends. Too, group daydreaming is enjoyable. One person can to begin a story and the others can add to it. If you start tomorrow, you will have years of excitement ahead of you.

Now look at the paragraph on page 143 carefully. Check it for:

1. Content
   a. Is the paragraph interesting?
   b. Does the paragraph give good reasons for participating in the activity?

2. Organization
   a. Does the paragraph answer the questions *what?*, *who?*, *where?*, *when?*, *how?*, and *why?*
   b. Does the topic sentence make the reader interested in the paragraph?

3. Cohesion and style
   a. Did the writer repeat the name of the activity and refer to it with the pronoun *it* or *this* appropriately?
   b. Did the writer use the pronoun *you* to refer to people in general?
   c. Did the writer use adjectives + infinitive complements correctly?
   d. Did the writer use gerunds correctly?

4. Correct form
   a. Did the writer use correct superlative forms?
   b. Did the writer use other forms correctly?

Discuss the corrections you made with other students.

Editing Your Writing

Now edit the paragraph you wrote. Check it for content, organization, cohesion, style, and form.

Writing the Second Draft

After you edit your paragraph, rewrite it neatly. Use good handwriting and correct form.

PART IV. COMMUNICATING THROUGH WRITING

Give your paragraph to your teacher for comments.

Sharing

Some students can read their paragraphs aloud for the class. Are there any activities students are interested in? Would the class like to plan a class trip or activity based on the recommendations?

Using Feedback

Look at your teacher's comments. If you don't understand something, ask about it.

Read another student's paragraph and write two or three sentences about it. Tell why you thought it was interesting and write why you would or wouldn't like to participate in the activity.

12
YOU, THE CONSUMER

PART I. GETTING READY TO WRITE

Exploring Ideas

Look at these pictures, which show people who have just bought something that they are not happy with. What's wrong in each picture?

Now discuss these questions in small groups.

1. Have you ever bought something from a store and been disappointed with it? What was the item? What was wrong with it?

2. What did you do? Did you keep the item? Did you take it back? If you took it back, what happened?

Building Vocabulary

Add other words you used in your discussion to this list.

Nouns	Verbs	Adjectives	Other
refund	refund	defective	_____
receipt	exchange	dissatisfied	_____
guarantee	return	guaranteed	_____
warranty	complain	_____	_____
complaint department	purchase	_____	_____
manager	_____	_____	_____
_____	_____	_____	_____
_____	_____	_____	_____
_____	_____	_____	_____

Organizing Ideas

Determining the Characteristics of an Effective Letter of Complaint

You are going to write a letter of complaint about something that you bought that you are dissatisfied with.

The well-written letter of complaint should:

1. state the problem clearly and simply
2. give definite dates, order numbers, etc.
3. suggest a solution
4. be polite
5. be addressed to the person who will be able to do something about the problem

Jaime Martinez bought a kitchen appliance from a mail order catalog. Read his letter of complaint. Where does he need to add details?

Dear Sir,

   The other day I ordered an electric frying pan from your catalog. When it arrived, it didn't work. Please refund my money.

                               Sincerely

                               Jaime Martinez
                               Jaime Martinez

Although it is important to include enough information, you should be careful *not* to include unnecessary details.

   Marie Wolpert bought a suitcase at a large department store. She is unhappy with it and would like to return it. Here are notes for a letter that she is writing to the department manager. Read them and draw a line through any unnecessary details.

1. Skyway suitcase
2. 30″ × 45″
3. light blue
4. purchased June 17
5. paid cash
6. reduced from $50 to $42
7. handle broke on trip to Buffalo

8. handle broke first time used
9. called the store
10. spoke with the manager of luggage department on July 15
11. manager said no refunds or exchanges on sale items
12. manager's name Simon Grey
13. would like to exchange suitcase

Think of a time when you bought something that you were dissatisfied with. Make a list of the important details.

_____

_____

_____

_____

_____

_____

_____

_____

_____

_____

_____

Now exchange lists with another student in your class. Can you understand the situation? Has he or she included all the important information? Has he or she included any unnecessary details?

PART II. DEVELOPING WRITING SKILLS

Developing Cohesion and Style

Using Past Participles as Adjectives

Many adjectives are the same as the past participle of a verb. Look at these sentences:

> *Examples:* When the bowl arrived, it was *broken*. (past participle that functions as an adjective)
>
> Oh no! I've *broken* the bowl! (past participle that is part of the present perfect tense: *have broken*)

Now look at these verbs and tell what their past participles will be. Then use the past participles as adjectives in a sentence.

Example: stain *stained*
The blouse looks stained with tomato juice.

1. smash

2. open

3. destroy

4. tear

5. fade

6. dissatisfy

7. rip _____

8. scratch _____

Using Formal Language

A business letter should be formal and polite. People generally use more formal vocabulary in business letters than in letters to friends. Here are some more formal alternatives for words you already know. Read the sentences and try to guess what the italicized words mean.

1. On May 12, I *purchased* a pair of shoes at your store.

2. I have been waiting for a refund for three weeks, but I haven't *received* it yet.

3. Therefore, I am *requesting* a refund.

To make a business letter polite, you should try not be too direct. For example, instead of "You should refund my money," you might say, "I feel that the company should refund my money."

Another way to make a business letter more polite is to use the words *would* and *could* when you are making a request. Instead of "Please return my deposit," you might say, "Would (could) you please return my deposit?" or "I would appreciate it if you would return my deposit."

Look at this letter of complaint. Rewrite it to make it more formal and more polite.

Dear Sir,

Last week I bought a set of six glasses in your store. You sent them to my home. When I got the package, four of the glasses were broken. I want a refund for all six glasses. Send it to me soon.

Sincerely,

Kate Collins

Kate Collins

_____

_____

_____

_____

_____

_____

_____

_____

_____

_____

Using Correct Form

Following the Format of a Business Letter

HEADING {
15 South Cedar Street
Boston, Massachusetts 02214
January 11, 19XX

Manager
Sales Department
Universal Publishing Company
1523 Castleton Boulevard
New York, New York 10027
} **INSIDE ADDRESS**

Dear Sir: **SALUTATION**

On December 15, 19XX I ordered one copy of <u>The United States in Pictures</u> by Jerome Massanti. I } **BODY** included a check for the full price of the book, $18.97 plus $2.00 for shipping and handling charges. On December 27, 1984 I received a letter from your order department that said that the book would not be available until May of this year. The letter also said that if I wanted a refund, I could have it. On January 2, 1985 I wrote and asked them to refund my $20.97. It is now four weeks later and I still have not received my refund.   **}** **BODY**

    Would you please look into this matter for me? I have often ordered books from your company and would like to continue doing business with you.

CLOSING   Very truly yours,

Simon La Grande

SIGNATURE   Simon La Grande

HEADING: The heading tells where and when the writer wrote the letter. It should be in the upper right-hand corner of the first page, an inch or more from the top. The heading should contain the writer's complete address:

> number and street
> city, state or province, postal code
> country (if the letter is sent out of the country)

It should also contain the date.

INSIDE ADDRESS: The inside address contains the name and the address of the person or company you are writing to. It is usually on the left two spaces below the date. If you know the name and title of the person, you should include them. For example:

> David Pearson, Manager
> Sales Department
>
> Margaret McGraw, Customer Relations

SALUTATION: The salutation or greeting should be two spaces below the inside address. The most common salutations are:

> Dear Sir or Madam:
> Dear Mr. Fraser:
> Dear Ms. Kaplan:
> Dear Mrs. Foster:

BODY: The body of the letter begins two spaces below the salutation. You should indent the paragraphs. There should be a margin of at least one inch on both sides of the paper, at the top, and at the bottom. If your letter is very short, you should make your margins larger.

CLOSING AND SIGNATURE: The closing is two spaces below the last line of the body. A comma follows it. Capitalize only the first word. Some common ways to close formal letters are:

> Very truly yours,
> Yours truly,
> Sincerely yours,

Sign the letter about one-half inch below the closing. Then type or print your name under your signature.

Put the following information in the correct place in the letter form that follows it. Add commas where necessary.

Customer Service Department, Sullivan Office Furniture

Company, 1432 Bradley Boulevard, Muskegon, Michigan, 49441

July 12, 1985

Dear Sir:

157 John Street, New York, New York 10038

Yours sincerely

Jane Fulton

Jane Fulton

Office Manager

XXXXXXXXXXXXXXXXXXXXXXXXXXXXXXXXXXXXXXXXXXXXXXXXXXXXX
XXXXXXXXXXXXXXXXXXXXXXXXXXXXXXXXXXXXXXXXXXXXXXXXXXXXX

XXXXXXXXXXXXXXXXXXXXXXXXXXXXXXXXXXXXXXXXXXXXXXXXXXXXX

XXXXXXXXXXXXXXXXXXXXXXXXXXXXXXXXXXXXXXXXXXXXXXXXXXXXX

XXXXXXXXXXXXXXXXXXXXXXXXXXXXXXXXXXXXXXXXXXXXXXXXXXXXX
XXXXXXXXXXXXXXXXXXXXXXXXXXXXXXXXXXXXXXXXXXXXXXXXXXXXX

PART III. WRITING AND EDITING

Writing the First Draft

Now write your letter of complaint.

Editing Practice

Edit this letter and rewrite it correctly.

February 24, 19XX

125 South Street
Brattleboro
Vermont 05301

David Drew
Manager Repair Dept.
Empire Typewriter
Company
309 Fourth St,
Pipe Creek, Texas 78063

dear manager

last month I sent my typewriter to you for repairs because it wasn't working correctly. I got it for my birthday. You repair department promise to send to me in two weeks. I still haven't gotten it back. I need my typewriter now. You had better tell them to repair it and send it to me quickly.

David Wright

Now look at the letter carefully. Check it for:

1. Content
   a. Did the writer explain the problem clearly?

2. Organization
   a. Did the writer include all the necessary details?
   b. Did the writer include any unnecessary details?

3. Cohesion and style
   a. Did the writer use formal language?
   b. Did the writer use polite language?

4. Grammar
   a. Did the writer use correct verb forms?

5. Correct form
   a. Did the writer use the correct business letter format?

Discuss the corrections you made with other students.

Editing Your Writing

Now edit the letter you wrote. Check it for content, organization, cohesion, style, and form.

Writing the Second Draft

After you edit your paragraph, rewrite it neatly. Use good handwriting and correct form.

PART IV. COMMUNICATING THROUGH WRITING

Give your paragraph to your teacher for comments.

Sharing

Exchange letters with another student. Pretend you are the person who received the letter and decide what you will do about the complaint. Discuss your decision with the writer.

Using Feedback

Look at your teacher's comments. If you don't understand something, ask about it.

APPENDICES

APPENDIX 1

Spelling Rules for Adding Endings

Rules for Adding Endings That Begin with Vowels (ed, ing, er, est)

1. For words ending in a silent *e*, drop the *e* and add the ending.

   like → lik**ed**   make → mak**ing**   safe → saf**er**   fine → fin**est**

2. For one-syllable words ending in a single vowel and a single consonant, double the final consonant.

   ba**t** → bat**ted**   ru**n** → run**ning**   fa**t** → fat**ter**   ho**t** → hot**test**

3. Don't double the final consonant when the word has two final consonants or two vowels before a final consonant.

   pi**ck** → pick**ed**   si**ng** → sing**ing**   clean → clean**er**   cool → cool**est**

4. For words of two or more syllables that end in a single vowel and a single consonant, double the final consonant if the word is accented on the final syllable.

   refer′ → refer**red**   begin′ → begin**ning**

5. For words of two or more syllables that end in a single vowel and a single consonant, make no change if the word isn't accented on the final syllable.

   trável → travel**ed**   fócus → focus**ed**

6. For words ending in a consonant and *y*, change the *y* to *i* and add the ending unless the ending begins with *i*.

   study → stud**ied**   dirty → dirt**ier**   sunny → sunn**iest**
   study → stud**ying**   hurry → hurr**ying**

7. For words ending in a vowel and *y*, make no change before adding the ending.

   play → play**ed**   stay → stay**ing**

Rules for Adding Endings That Begin with Consonants (ly, ment)

8. When words end in a silent *e*, make no change when adding endings that begin with consonants.

   fin**e** → fine**ly**   stat**e** → state**ment**

9. When words end in a consonant and *y*, change the *y* to *i* before adding the ending.

   hap**py** → happ**ily**   mer**ry** → merr**iment**

Rules for Adding a Final s to Nouns and Verbs

10. Generally, add the *s* without making changes.

    sit → sit**s**   dance → dance**s**   play → play**s**   book → book**s**

11. If a word ends in a consonant and *y*, change the *y* to *i* and add *es*.

    mar**ry** → marr**ies**   stu**dy** → stud**ies**   cher**ry** → cherr**ies**

12. If a word ends in *s, x, ch, sh,* or *z*, add *es*.

    boss → boss**es**   mix → mix**es**   chur**ch** → church**es**
    cash → cash**es**   fizz → fizz**es**

13. If a word ends in *o*, sometimes add *es* and sometimes add *s*.

    tomat**o** → tomato**es**   potat**o** → potato**es**
    pian**o** → piano**s**   radi**o** → radio**s**

14. If a word ends in *f* or *fe*, generally drop the *f* or *fe* and add *ves*.

    kni**fe** → kni**ves**   wi**fe** → wi**ves**   li**fe** → li**ves**   loa**f** → loa**ves**
    Exceptions: sa**fe** → sa**fes**   puff → puff**s**   roof → roof**s**

APPENDIX 2

Capitalization Rules

First Words

1. Capitalize the first word of every sentence.

   I live in Rome.   **W**ho is it?

2. Capitalize the first word of a quotation.

   He said, "**M**y name is Paul."   Jenny asked, "**W**hen is the party?"

Personal Names

3. Capitalize names of people including initials and titles of address.

   Mrs. **J**ones   **I**ndira **G**andhi   **J**ohn **F**. **K**ennedy

4. Capitalize family words if used alone or followed by a name.

Let's go, **D**ad.   Where's **G**randma?   She's at **A**unt Lucy's.

5. Don't capitalize family words if used with a possessive pronoun or article.

my **u**ncle   her **m**other   our **g**randparents   an **a**unt

6. Capitalize the pronoun *I*.

I have a book.   She's bigger than **I** am.

7. Capitalize names of God.

God   **A**llah   **J**esus **C**hrist

8. Capitalize the names of nationalities, races, peoples, and religions.

Arab   **O**riental   **C**hicano   **M**uslim

9. Generally, don't capitalize occupations.

I am a **s**ecretary.   She wants to be a **l**awyer.

Place Names

10. Capitalize the names of countries, states, provinces, and cities.

Mexico   **N**ew **Y**ork   **O**ntario   **T**okyo

11. Capitalize the names of oceans, lakes, rivers, islands, and mountains.

the **A**tlantic **O**cean   **L**ake **C**omo   the **A**mazon
Belle **I**sle   **M**t. **E**verest

12. Capitalize the names of geographical areas.

the **S**outh   the **E**ast **C**oast   **A**sia   **A**ntarctica

13. Don't capitalize directions if they aren't names of geographical areas.

He lives **e**ast of Toronto.   They traveled **s**outhwest.

14. Capitalize names of parks, buildings, and streets.

Central **P**ark   the **S**ears **B**uilding   **O**xford **R**oad

Time Words

15. Capitalize names of days and months.

Monday   **F**riday   **J**anuary   **M**arch

16. Capitalize names of holidays and historical events.

Christmas   **N**ew **Y**ear's **D**ay   **I**ndependence **D**ay   **W**orld **W**ar II

17. Don't capitalize names of seasons.

spring   **s**ummer   **f**all   **w**inter

Titles

18. Capitalize the first word and all important words of titles of books, magazines, newspapers, and articles.

Interactions   *Newsweek*
The New York Times   "Rock Music Today"

19. Capitalize the first word and all important words of names of movies, plays, radio programs, and television programs.

    Star **W**ars   **A** *Chorus* **L**ine   "**N**ews **R**oundup"   "**F**ame"

20. Don't capitalize articles (*a, an, the*), conjunctions (*but, and, or*), and short prepositions (*of, with, in, on, for*) unless they are the first word of a title.

    The Life **of** Thomas Edison   War **a**nd Peace   Death **of a** Salesman

Names of Organizations

21. Capitalize the names of organizations, government groups, and businesses.

    International **S**tudent **A**ssociation   the **S**enate   **G**estetner

22. Capitalize trade names, but do not capitalize the name of the product.

    IBM typewriter   **T**oyota hatchback   **K**ellogg's cereal

Other

23. Capitalize the names of languages.

    Spanish   **T**hai   **F**rench   **J**apanese

24. Don't capitalize school subjects unless they are the names of languages or are followed by a number.

    geometry   music   **E**nglish   **A**rabic   **B**iology 306

APPENDIX 3

Punctuation Rules

Period

1. Use a period after a statement or command.

    We are studying English.   Open your books to Chapter 3.

2. Use a period after most abbreviations.

    Mr.   Ms.   Dr.   Ave.   etc.   U.S.   t.v.
    Exceptions: UN   NATO   IBM

3. Use a period after initials.

    H. G. Wells   Mrs. H. R. Hammond

Question Mark

4. Use a question mark after (not before) questions.

    Where are you going?   Is he here yet?

5. In a direct quotation, the question mark goes before the quotation marks.

    He asked, "What's your name?"

Exclamation Point

6. Use an exclamation point after exclamatory sentences or phrases.

> I won the lottery!　　　Be quiet!　　　Wow!

Comma

7. Use a comma before a conjunction (*and, or, so, but*) that separates two independent clauses.

> She wanted to go to work, so she decided to take an English course.
> He wasn't happy in that apartment, but he didn't have the money to move.

8. Don't use a comma before a conjunction that separates two phrases that aren't complete sentences.

> She worked in the library and studied at night.
> Do you want to go to a movie or stay home?

9. Use a comma before an introductory clause or phrase (generally if it is five or more words long).

> After a beautiful wedding ceremony, they had a reception in her mother's home.
> If you want to write well, you should practice writing almost every night.

10. Use a comma to separate interrupting expressions from the rest of a sentence.

> Do you know, by the way, what time dinner is?
> Many of the students, I found out, stayed on campus during the summer.

11. Use a comma after transitional expressions.

> In addition, he stole all her jewelry.
> However, he left the t.v.

12. Use a comma to separate names of people in direct address from the rest of a sentence.

> Jane, have you seen Paul?
> We aren't sure, Mrs. Shapiro, where he is.

13. Use a comma after *yes* and *no* in answers.

> Yes, he was here a minute ago.
> No, I haven't.

14. Use a comma to separate items in a series.

> We have coffee, tea, and milk.
> He looked in the refrigerator, on the shelves, and in the cupboard.

15. Use a comma to separate an appositive from the rest of a sentence.

> Mrs. Sampson, his English teacher, gave him a good recommendation.
> Would you like to try a taco, a delicious Mexican food?

16. If a date or address has two or more parts, use a comma after each part.

> I was born on June 5, 1968.
> The house at 230 Seventh Street, Miami, Florida, is for sale.

17. Use a comma to separate contrasting information from the rest of a sentence.

It wasn't Maria, but Parvin, who was absent.
Bring your writing book, not your reading book.

18. Use a comma to separate quotations from the rest of a sentence.

He asked, "What are we going to do?"
"I'm working downtown," he said.

19. Use a comma to separate two or more adjectives that each modify the noun alone.

She was an intelligent, beautiful actress. (*intelligent* and *beautiful* actress)
Eat those delicious green peas. (*delicious* modifies *green peas*)

20. Use a comma to separate nonrestrictive clauses from the rest of a sentence. A nonrestrictive clause gives more information about the noun it describes, but it isn't needed to identify the noun. Clauses after proper names are nonrestrictive and require commas.

Flashdance, which is about a factory worker and dancer, is my favorite movie.
Jennifer Beals, who doesn't dance in the movie, is the star of *Flashdance.*

Quotation Marks

21. Use quotation marks at the beginning and end of exact quotations. Other punctuation marks go before the end quotation marks.

He said, "I'm going to Montreal."
"How are you?" he asked.

22. Use quotation marks before and after titles of stories, articles, songs, and television programs. Periods and commas go before the final quotation marks, while question marks and exclamation points normally go after them.

Do you like to watch "Dallas" on television?
My favorite song is "Let It Be."
Do you like the story "Gift of the Magi"?

Apostrophes

23. Use apostrophes in contractions.

don't   it's   we've   they're

24. Use an apostrophe to make possessive nouns.

Singular: Jerry's   my boss's
Plural: the children's   the Smiths'

Underlining

25. Underline the titles of books, magazines, newspapers, plays, and movies.

I am reading <u>One Hundred Years of Solitude.</u>
Did you like the movie <u>Star Wars?</u>

CHAPTER 1 FEEDBACK SHEET

Student Name _____ Date _____

Personal reaction:

_____

_____

_____

_____

_____

Chapter checklist:

	Good	Needs Work
Content		
1. Level of interest of information	☐	☐
Organization		
1. All information about one person	☐	☐
2. Order of sentences	☐	☐
3. Topic sentence	☐	☐
Cohesion and Style		
1. Connecting sentences with *and, so, but*	☐	☐
2. Use of *also*	☐	☐
Grammar		
1. Present tense verbs	☐	☐
2. Pronouns	☐	☐
Form		
1. Paragraph form	☐	☐
2. Spelling	☐	☐
3. Handwriting	☐	☐

Other comments:

_____

_____

_____

_____

_____

CHAPTER 2 FEEDBACK SHEET

Student Name _____ Date _____

Personal reaction:

_____

_____

_____

_____

_____

Chapter checklist:

	Good	Needs Work
Content		
1. Use of interesting adjectives	☐	☐
Organization		
1. Order of sentences	☐	☐
Cohesion and Style		
1. Connecting sentences	☐	☐
2. Verb forms	☐	☐
3. Article use	☐	☐
Grammar		
1. Subject-verb agreement	☐	☐
2. Pronoun use	☐	☐
3. Placement of adjectives	☐	☐
Form		
1. Paragraph form	☐	☐
2. Spelling of present participles	☐	☐

Other comments:

_____

_____

_____

_____

_____

CHAPTER 3 FEEDBACK SHEET

Student Name _____ Date _____

Personal reaction:

_____

_____

_____

_____

_____

Chapter checklist:

	Good	Needs Work
Content		
1. Interesting information	☐	☐
2. Clear information	☐	☐
Organization		
1. Topic sentence	☐	☐
2. All information about the holiday	☐	☐
3. Order of sentences	☐	☐
Cohesion and Style		
1. Use of appositives	☐	☐
2. Connecting sentences	☐	☐
3. Use of *such as*	☐	☐
Grammar		
1. Present tense verbs	☐	☐
2. Count and noncount nouns	☐	☐
Form		
1. Paragraph form	☐	☐
2. Spelling of words with -*s* endings	☐	☐
3. Commas with appositives	☐	☐

Other comments:

_____

_____

_____

_____

CHAPTER 4 FEEDBACK SHEET

Student Name _____ Date _____

Personal reaction:

_____

_____

_____

_____

_____

Chapter checklist:

	Good	Needs Work
Content		
1. Interesting activities	☐	☐
2. Clear directions	☐	☐
Organization		
1. Each paragraph about a different topic	☐	☐
2. Salutation and closing	☐	☐
Cohesion and Style		
1. Verb tenses	☐	☐
2. Prepositions	☐	☐
3. Use of *there* and *it*	☐	☐
Grammar		
1. Verb forms	☐	☐
2. Subject-verb agreement	☐	☐
Form		
1. Date	☐	☐
2. Salutation	☐	☐
3. Indentation of paragraphs	☐	☐
4. Closing	☐	☐

Other comments:

_____

_____

_____

_____

CHAPTER 5 FEEDBACK SHEET

Student Name _____ Date _____

Personal reaction:

_____
_____
_____
_____

Chapter checklist:

	Good	Needs Work
Content		
1. Interesting information	☐	☐
2. Important information	☐	☐
Organization		
1. Topic sentence	☐	☐
2. All sentences about one topic	☐	☐
3. Order of sentences	☐	☐
Cohesion and Style		
1. Past-tense verbs	☐	☐
2. Combining sentences with time words	☐	☐
3. Combining sentences with *and, but, so*	☐	☐
Grammar		
1. Nouns	☐	☐
2. Pronouns	☐	☐
3. Articles	☐	☐
4. Sentence structure (no fragments)	☐	☐
Form		
1. Paragraph form	☐	☐
2. Capitalization of title	☐	☐
3. Punctuation with combined sentences	☐	☐
4. Spelling	☐	☐

Other comments:

_____
_____
_____

CHAPTER 6 FEEDBACK SHEET

Student Name _____ Date _____

Personal reaction:

_____
_____
_____
_____
_____

Chapter checklist:

	Good	Needs Work
Content		
1. Clear story	☐	☐
2. Important information	☐	☐
Organization		
1. Use of time words	☐	☐
2. Title	☐	☐
Cohesion and Style		
1. Varied time expressions	☐	☐
2. Description	☐	☐
3. Quotations	☐	☐
Grammar		
1. Past-tense verbs	☐	☐
2. Present-continuous tense verbs	☐	☐
3. Sentence structure (no fragments)	☐	☐
Form		
1. Use of commas	☐	☐
2. Use of quotation marks	☐	☐

Other comments:

_____
_____
_____
_____
_____

CHAPTER 7 FEEDBACK SHEET

Student Name _____ Date _____

Personal reaction:

_____

_____

_____

_____

_____

Chapter checklist:

	Good	Needs Work
Content		
1. Interesting information	☐	☐
2. Reasons and examples	☐	☐
Organization		
1. Topic sentence	☐	☐
2. All information about one topic	☐	☐
3. Amount of information	☐	☐
Cohesion and Style		
1. Relative clauses	☐	☐
2. Use of *in addition*	☐	☐
3. Use of *for example*	☐	☐
4. Use of *however*	☐	☐
5. Use of synonyms	☐	☐
6. Verb tenses	☐	☐
Grammar		
1. Use of noun forms	☐	☐
Form		
1. Use of commas	☐	☐

Other comments:

_____

_____

_____

_____

CHAPTER 8 FEEDBACK SHEET

Student Name _____ Date _____

Personal reaction:

_____

_____

_____

_____

_____

Chapter checklist:

	Good	Needs Work
Content		
1. Interesting title	☐	☐
2. Interesting information	☐	☐
Organization		
1. Use of details	☐	☐
2. Topic sentence	☐	☐
3. Concluding sentence	☐	☐
4. Clear presentation	☐	☐
Cohesion and Style		
1. Verb tenses	☐	☐
2. Use of appositives	☐	☐
Grammar		
1. Sentence structure (no fragments)	☐	☐
Form		
1. Capitalization of title	☐	☐
2. Use of commas	☐	☐

Other comments:

_____

_____

_____

_____

_____

CHAPTER 9 FEEDBACK SHEET

Student Name _____ Date _____

Personal reaction:

_____

_____

_____

_____

_____

Chapter checklist:

	Good	Needs Work
Content		
1. Interesting information	☐	☐
Organization		
1. Topic sentence	☐	☐
2. Well-organized sentences	☐	☐
3. Concluding sentence	☐	☐
Cohesion and Style		
1. Verb tenses	☐	☐
2. Use of *however*	☐	☐
3. Use of *also*	☐	☐
4. Use of *in addition*	☐	☐
5. Use of *in fact*	☐	☐
6. Use of *so that*	☐	☐
Grammar		
1. Verb forms	☐	☐
Form		
1. Use of commas	☐	☐
2. Spelling of verb forms	☐	☐
3. Capitalization	☐	☐

Other comments:

_____

_____

_____

_____

CHAPTER 10 FEEDBACK SHEET

Student Name _____ Date _____

Personal reaction:

_____

_____

_____

_____

_____

Chapter checklist:

	Good	Needs Work
Content		
1. Interesting information	☐	☐
Organization		
1. Order of information	☐	☐
2. Amount of information	☐	☐
Cohesion and Style		
1. Use of quantifiers	☐	☐
2. Use of *in addition to*	☐	☐
3. Use of *besides*	☐	☐
4. Use of *another*	☐	☐
5. Use of *the first,* etc.	☐	☐
6. Use of nonrestrictive relative clauses	☐	☐
Grammar		
1. Sentence structure (no fragments)	☐	☐
Form		
1. Capitalization of title	☐	☐
2. Use of commas with nonrestrictive relative clauses	☐	☐

Other comments:

_____

_____

_____

_____

CHAPTER 11 FEEDBACK SHEET

Student Name _____ Date _____

Personal reaction:

_____

_____

_____

_____

_____

Chapter checklist:

	Good	Needs Work
Content		
1. Interesting information	☐	☐
2. Use of reasons	☐	☐
Organization		
1. Complete information	☐	☐
2. Topic sentence	☐	☐
Cohesion and Style		
1. Use of *it* and *this*	☐	☐
2. Use of the general *you*	☐	☐
3. Use of adjectives + infinitive complements	☐	☐
4. Use of gerunds	☐	☐
Grammar		
1. Verb forms	☐	☐
Form		
1. Superlative forms	☐	☐

Other comments:

_____

_____

_____

_____

_____

CHAPTER 12 FEEDBACK SHEET

Student Name _____ Date _____

Personal reaction:

_____

_____

_____

_____

_____

Chapter checklist:

	Good	Needs Work
Content		
1. Clear presentation of information	☐	☐
Organization		
1. Amount of information	☐	☐
Cohesion and Style		
1. Use of formal language	☐	☐
2. Polite tone	☐	☐
Grammar		
1. Verb forms	☐	☐
Form		
1. Neatness	☐	☐
2. Date	☐	☐
3. Inside address	☐	☐
4. Salutation	☐	☐
5. Closing	☐	☐

Other comments:

_____

_____

_____

_____